The Literature of the Woodwind Quintet

Compiled by
HARRY B. PETERS
Professor in Music
University of Wisconsin, Madison

The Scarecrow Press, Inc.
Metuchen, N.J.   1971

Dedicated with Pleasure
to my colleagues of the Wingra Woodwind Quintet
Robert Cole, Glenn Bowen, John Barrows, Richard Lottridge

Table of Contents

Acknowledgment

In addition to the authors whose research produced many of my sources, my deepest gratitude goes to my colleagues, John Barrows, Glenn Bowen, Robert Cole and Richard Lottridge for participating in playing and annotating the quintets; to William Bunce, Fine Arts Librarian of the University of Wisconsin, for his many suggestions and vast knowledge of library resources; and to Edgar Kirk, Ron Hounsell, and Gwynn McPeek for generously researching their local areas.

Preface

This repertoire of woodwind music for quintet has been compiled from many sources: music publishers' and dealers' catalogues, reference books, other bibliographies and reports from woodwind players throughout the country. At first, the only intention was to compile a list of original compositions for quintet. However, because such a large number of excellent arrangements exist, it seemed valuable to include them as well. If there are inadvertent omissions, it will more likely be of arrangements than of original compositions. For example, John Barrows, a member of our Wingra Woodwind Quintet, informs me he knows of no less than four hundred and ninety-five arrangements for quintet by the now deceased Ross Taylor, and only a few are published.

The compilation is arranged with standard quintet repertoire followed by separate lists of music for woodwind quintet plus one, two, three, four and five additional performers. It is organized to aid in the selection of music for whatever instrument (or instruments) the additional performer (or performers) play.

In cases where a dealer's catalogue was used, items such as the publisher or arranger are not always included. In this instance the name of the dealer is listed and it is assumed the music is procurable from him. In cross-checking one source against another, conflicting data and misspellings have sometimes been found. Thus, occasionally a work may be listed with more than one title. Rather than eliminate a questionable title, all are reported. Data that could not be confirmed is indicated as questionable.

"Wind Quintet" is usually taken to mean woodwind quintet by librarians and researchers. Fuvosotos is the Hungarian term for woodwind quintet.

In consultation with the other members of the Wingra Quintet of the University of Wisconsin, the author has undertaken to add remarks about some of the quintets. Not all of the compositions performed or read were evaluated. In some cases we preferred to withhold comment, and in some instances we neglected to discuss and record our comments while they were still fresh in our minds.

The annotations attempt to: 1) indicate the length of the work; 2) estimate the overall difficulty; 3) describe its idiom, and 4) give an occasional judgment concerning the impact of the music on the performers or the audience. Symbols have been used to indicate relative lengths of works and performing quality or appropriateness. The single letter (A or B) indicates a short composition. Double letters (AA or BB) denote a work of substantial length, usually containing several movements. A (or AA) recommends the piece as fully worthy of inclusion on any major program. B (or BB) commends the piece as one which might possibly be included. The number that follows the letter abbreviations gives some idea of the composite difficulty of the music: 6 represents the most difficult, 1 the least. Thus, a piece annotated AA-6 is a lengthy piece, worthy of performance on a major recital, difficult to perform either technically, ensemble-wise, or both.

Abbreviations

arr.	arranged
c.	circa
coll.	college
ed.	edition
found.	foundation
G (capital)	G major
g	g minor
horn	French horn
lib.	library
maj.	major
min.	minor
Ms.	manuscript
Ms. ?	unknown if in manuscript or published form
op.	opus
priv.	private
pub.	published
Univ.	University

Abbreviations Under Annotation

6:22   6 minutes, 22 seconds

A, B.   short composition

AA, BB   composition of length, usually
                                several movements

1-6   degree of difficulty. (1) being
                                least difficult

    (see preface for full explanation)

ACA	American Composers Alliance, 2121 Broadway, New York 10023.
	Ahn and Simrock (via Schirmer), Schutzenhofstrasse 4, Weisbaden, 62.
	Alcove (via Western International Music).
	Alkor Edition, Kassel.
Am. Music Center	American Music Center, Agents for American Music Edition, Arrow Music, New Music Edition, 250 W. 57th St., New York 10019.
ASCAP	American Society of Composers, Authors and Publishers, 30 Rockefeller Plaza, New York 10020.
AMP	Associated Music Publishers, 1 W. 47th St., New York 10036.
	Andraud, Albert J. (deceased), now Southern Music Co.
	Andre, Joann, Frankfurterstrasse 28, Offenbach a. M.
	Anglo-Soviet Music Press, Ltd., 295 Regent St., London, W 1.
	Arrow Music Press, 250 W. 57th St., New York 10019.
	Ars Nova (via Elkan-Vogel).
	Ars Viva Verlag (Hermann Scherchen) now Schott (via AMP), Mainz.
	Artia Edition, POB 790, Prague I.
	A Tempo Verlag, Vienna.
	Augener, Ltd., 18 Gt. Marlborough St., London, W 1.
	Avant Music, 2859 Holt Ave., Los Angeles 90034.
Bar.	Bärenreiter Verlag, 1) Wilhelmshohe Heinrich Schutz Allee, 35, Kassel; 2) Gt. Titchfield St., London, W 1; 3) 250 W. 57th St., New York 10019.
	Barnhouse, C. L., High Ave., at L. St., Oskaloosa, Iowa 52577.

Baron, M. & Co., 1) 136 Chatsword Rd.,
    London, NW 2; 2) 8 W. 45th St., New
    York 10036.
Baudoux, Paris.
Baxter-Northrup (now Keystone Music
    Service).
Belwin-Mills Publishing Corp. 250 Maple Ave.,
    Rockville Center, L. I., New York 11570.
Benjamin, Anton J., 1) Werderstrasse 44,
    Hamburg, 13; 2) 239 Shaftesbury Ave.,
    London, W. C. 2.
Birchard, C. C., 221 Columbus Ave.,
    Boston, Mass. 02100.
Birnbach, Richard, Schutzenstrasse 6,
    Berlin, S. W. 68.
Blake, Whitney, New York.

BMI   Broadcast Music Inc., 1) 16 Gould St.,
               Toronto 2, Ontario; 2) 589 Fifth Ave.,
               New York 10019.
               Bohm, Anton & Sohn, Lange Gasse 26,
               Augsburg.
               Bomart Music Corp., Hillsdale, New York
               12529.

B & H   Boosey and Hawkes. 1) Bonn; 2) 295
               Regent St., London W 1; 3) Oceanside,
               New York 11572.
               Bosworth & Co. 1) Berlin; 2) 14-18 Heddon
               St., London W 1.

B & B   Bote und Bock, Hardenbergstrasse, 9a, Char-
               lottenburg 2, Berlin.
               Bourne, Inc., 136 W. 52nd St., New York
               10019.

Br. & H   Breitkopf and Hartel. 1) 25 W. 45th St.,
               New York 10036; 2) Karlstrasse 10,
               Leipzig C1; 3) Burgstrasse 6,
               Wiesbaden 1.
               Briegel, Geo. F., unknown.

Brod. & Wilk   Broderip & Wilkinson, London.
               Broekmans en Van Poppel (via Elkan
               Vogel), van Baerlestraat 92, Amsterdam.
               Brogneaux Edition (via Baron), 73 Paul
               Jansonlaan, Brussels.
               Bromley, Hull.
               Broude Brothers, 56 W. 45th St., New
               York 10036.
               Buffet-Crampon, 18 Passage du Grand-
               Cerf, Paris 2.

Bulg. St.	Bulgarian State (Editura Musicala), Calea Victorici 41-43, Bucharest.
	Camara Music Publishers, 3505 Iroquois St., Detroit, Mich. 48214.
Can. Mus. Cent.	Canadian Music Center, 559 Avenue Rd., Toronto 5, Ontario.
	Carish, S. P. A. (via Baron; Mills), Via G. Fara 39, Milan.
CeDeBeM	Centre Belge de Documentation Musicale, rue de Commerce 3, Brussels.
	Cesky Hudebny Fond, Prague.
	Chappell and Co. 1) 50 New Bond St., London W 1; 2) 609 Fifth Ave., New York 10017.
	Chester, J. & W. (via Belwin-Mills), 11 Gt. Marlborough St., London W 1.
	Choudens (via Peters), 38 rue Jean-Mermoz, Paris.
	Colombo, Franco (formerly Ricordi), 16 W. 61st St., New York 10023.
	Composers Autograph Publications, Redondo Beach, Cal. 90277.
	Composers Facsimile Edition (ACA), 170 W. 74th St., New York 10023.
	Composers Press, Inc., 1211 Ditmas Ave., Brooklyn 11218.
Comp. Rec.	Composers Recording, Inc., New York.
	Concord Music (via Henri Elkan).
CMP	Consolidated Music Publishers (see ASCAP).
Cont. Mus. Proj.	Contemporary Music Project (Music-University Microfilms), 300 N. Zeeb Rd., Ann Arbor, Mich. 48106.
	Continental Edition, Prague.
	Cor Publishing Co., Massapequa, L. I., New York 11758.
	Cos Cobb Press
	Costallat and Cie. (via Baron), 60 Chausée d'Autin, Paris 9.
	Cotelle, Paris.
	Cubitt, W. D. and Son, London.
	Cundy Bettoney Co., 96 Bradlee St., Hyde Park, Boston 02136.
	Curci, Fratelli, Galleria del Corso 4, Milan.
	Curwen & Sons (via Schirmer), 29 Maiden Lane, London, W. C. 2.
	Curwin, Inc. (via Schirmer), 441 Abbotsford Rd., Philadelphia 19144.

Czech State Music (see Artia).

Dania Edition, Kronprinsessegade 26,
   Copenhagen.

Dehase Musikverlag, Dahlienstrasse 8,
   Munich 45.

Deiss et Crepin (via Salabert), 31 rue
   Meslay, Paris 3.

Demets (now Eschig) (via AMP), Paris.

Dennes

Derry Music Co.

de Wolfe (see Wolfe)

Doblinger, Ludwig.   1) Dorotheengasse 10,
   Vienna 1;   2) Adolfsalle 34, Wiesbaden.

Donemus, Jacob Obrechtstraat 51,
   Amsterdam.

Doran, 4938 Newcastle Ave. , Encino, Cal.

Douglas, Byron Pub. (via BMI?)

Drustvo | Drustvo Slavenskih Skadateljev, Ljubljana.

Durand and Cie (via Elkan-Vogel), 4 Place
   de la Madeleine, Paris 8.

Durdilly, V. , Paris.

Edicije Kompozitora Yugoslava, Yugoslavia.

Ed. "Science et Arts" | Edition d'etat "Science et Arts"
   Sophia.

Editura Musicala (Bulgarian State),
   Bucharest.

Edition Musica (see Zen Val), Budapest.

Ed. Mus. Transat. | Edition Musicales Transatlantiques, 14 Ave.
   Hoche, Paris 8.

Edition Kawe (via Musica Rara).

EMB | Educational Music Bureau, 30 E. Adams
   St. , Chicago 60603.

Edwards, J. W. , Inc. , Ann Arbor,
   Mich. 48100.

Elkan, Henri, 1316 Walnut St. ,
   Philadelphia 19107.

Elkan-Vogel, Inc. , 1716 Sansom St. ,
   Philadelphia 19103.

Enoch & Cie. 1) 27 Blvd. des Italiens,
   Paris 2;   2) 19 Hanover Square,
   London W 1.

Ensemble Music Press, East Northport,
   New York 11731.

Ensemble Publications, Box 98, Buffalo
   14222.

Eschig, Max and Cie, 48 Rue de Rome,
   Paris 8.

Eulenburg, Ernst, 48 Gt. Marlborough St.,
    London W 1.
Evette and Schaeffer, 108 rue d'Aboukir,
    Paris 2.
Finnish Music Council, Helsinki.
Fischer, Carl, 62 Cooper Square, New
    York 10003.
Fischer, J. and Bros., Harristown Rd.,
    Glen Rock, New Jersey 07400.
Fitzsimmons, H. T., 615 N. La Salle St.,
    Chicago 60610.
For. Sv. Ton. Foreningen Svenska Tonsattare, Tegnerlund-
    en 3, Stockholm Va.
Fox, Sam Publishing Co., 11 W. 60th St.,
    New York 10023.
Franco Colombo Inc. (Ricordi), 16 W. 61st
    St., New York 10023.
Franklin
Galaxy Music Corp., 2121 Broadway, New
    York 10023.
Gamble Hinged Music Co., 218 S. Wabash
    St., Chicago 60603.
Gamut, Cambridge, England.
Gaveaux, G. & S., Paris.
General Music Publishers, 414 E. 75th St.,
    New York 10021.
Giessel, C. Jr., Bayreuth.
Gobert, Paris.
Gombart, Augsburg.
Gornston, David, 117 W. 48th St., New
    York 10036.
Grosch, Phillip, Lisztstrasse 18, Munich 8.
Grus, 65 Rue de Miromesnil, Paris 8.
Hall-McCreary (now Schmitt, Hall and
    McCreary), Park Ave. at 6th St.,
    Minneapolis 55415.
Hamelle, J. (via Elkan-Vogel), 2 Blvd.
    Malesherbes, Paris 8.
Hansen, Leipzig.
Hansen Edition (also Wilhelmina), Eschen-
    heimer Landstrasse 12, Frankfurt
    a. M.
Hansen, Wilhelm, Gothersgade 9-11,
    Copenhagen.
Haslinger, Carl, Tuchlauben 11, Vienna 1.
Heinrichshofen, Postfach 141, Wilhelmshave.
Henn Edition, rue Petitot, Geneva 2.

Hentz, Paris.

Het Musiekfonds, Antwerp.

Heugel and Cie, 2 rue Vivienne, Paris 2.

Hinrichsen, Max, 10 Baches St., London
N 1.

Hofmeister (18th & 19th Century), Leipzig.

Hofmeister, Friederich. 1) Karlstrasse 10,
Leipzig; 2) Eppsteinerstrasse 43,
Frankfurt, a. M. 6.

Hohner, M., Trossingen, Wurtemberg.

Hud. Mat.   Hudebni Matice, Prague.

Huguenin, C.

Hullenhagen and Griehl, Hamburg.

Hungarian State Music, P.O. Box 149,
Budapest 62.

Ichthys, Moserstrasse, Stuttgart.

IMC   International Music Co., 509 Fifth Ave.,
New York 10017.

Interlochen Press, Interlochen, Mich.
49643.

Iris Verlag, Hernerstrasse 5,
Recklinghause.

Isr. League   Israel Composers League Publishers, P.O.
Box 11180, Tel Aviv.

Isr. Mus. Inst.   Israel Music Institute, 6 Ghen Blvd.,
P.O. Box 11253, Tel Aviv.

Isr. Mus. Pub.   Israel Music Publishers, 69 Ben Yehuda
St., Tel Aviv.

Israeli Publishing Agency, Tel Aviv.

Joshua Corp., 53 E. 54th St., New York,
10022.

Joubert, C. and Cie, 25 rue d'Hauteville,
Paris 10.

Jouve, Paris.

Joventuts Musicals, Barcelona.

Junne, Otto, Mitterstrasse 1, Munich 15.

Kahnt, C. F., In der Hofstatt 8,
Lindau i. B.

Kalmus, E. F., F. C. Box, Huntington
Station, L. I., New York 11746.

Kasparek, Munich.

Kendor, Delevan, Main & Grove Sts.,
New York 14042.

Kistner (19th Century), Leipzig.

Kistner and Siegel, Luisenstrasse 8,
Lippstadt.

Kjos, Neil A. Music Co., 223 W. Lake
St., Chicago 60606.

Kneusslin, F. , Amselstrasse 43, Basel 24.

Kultura, P. O. Box 149, Budapest.

Lacour, Paris.

Lafleur, J. R. & Son, 147 Wardour St. , London W 1.

Latin American Music Centre (c/o School of Music-Univ. of Indiana), Bloomington, Indiana 47401.

LeBlanc, Kenosha, Wis. 53140.

Leduc, 175 rue St. Honore, Paris 1.

Leeds, RKO Bldg. , Radio City, New York 10020.

Lehne, Hanover.

Le Loche

Lemoine, Henri and Cie, 17 rue Pigalle, Paris 9.

Lengnick, Alfred & Co. , 14 Sheraton St. , London W 1.

Les Nouvelles Edition, Paris.

Leuckhardt, F. E. C. , Bocklinstrasse 1, Munich 19.

Lienau, Robert, Lankwitzerstrasse 9, Lichterfelde, Berlin.

Litolff, Henri, Forsthausstrasse 101, Frankfort, a. M.

L'Oiseau Lyre Edition (also Lyre Bird Press, London), 122 rue de Grenelle, Paris 7.

Lopes Edition

Lyche, Harald, Kongensgatan 2, Oslo.

Mann. Musik.   Mannheimer Musikverlag, Richard Wagner-strasse 6, Mannheim 1.

Maurer, J. , 7 avenue du Verseau, Brussels.

Mc & M   McGinnis & Marx, 148 W. 67th St. , New York 10023.

Mercury Music Corp. (now Presser), 47 W. 63rd St. , New York 10023.

Merion Music, Inc. , Bryn Mawr, Penn. 19010.

Metropolis Editions, 24 avenue de France, Antwerp.

Mills, 1619 Broadway, New York 10019.

Mitteld. Verl.   Mitteldeutscher Verlag, Robert Blumstrasse 37, Halle, Saale.

M. J. Q. Music, 200 W. 57th St. , New York 10019.

Modern Edition (now Hans Wewerka), Franz Josephstrasse 2, Munich 13.

	Moseler, Karl Heinrich, Postfach 406, Wolfenbuttel.

Moseler, Karl Heinrich, Postfach 406,
   Wolfenbuttel.

Muller, Willy (Suddeutscher Musikverlag),
   Marzgasse 5, Heidelberg.

MCA   Music Corporation of America, 445 Park
   Ave. , New York 10022.

Musica Rara, 2 Gt. Marlborough St. ,
   London W 1.

Music Press, Inc. (see Presser), New
   York.

Mus. Pub. Hold.   Music Publishers Holding Corp. , 619 W.
   54th St. , New York 10019.

Musicus Edition, 333 W. 52nd St. , New
   York 10022.

New Music, 2305 Red River, Austin,
   Texas 78705.

New Wind Music Co. , 23 Ivor Place,
   London NW 1.

Noel, Pierre, Blvd. Poissoniere, Paris 9.

Nord. Musikfor.   Nordiska Musikforlagt, 35 Regeringsgatan,
   Stockholm Tull.

Norsk.   Norsk Musikforlag, Karl Johans Gate 39,
   Oslo.

Novello & Co. (via Belwin-Mills) Sevenoaks,
   Borough Green, Kent.

Odeon Music Edition

Oertel, J. , Hinuberstrasse 16, Hanover.

Oiseaulyre (see L'Oiseau Lyre), Paris.

Okra Music Corp. , 177 E. 87th St. , New
   York 10028.

Omega Music, 170 W. 44th St. , New York
   10036.

Orbis, Prague.

OUP; Oxford   Oxford University Press.   1) 44 Conduit St. ,
Univ. Press   London W 1;   2) 417 Fifth Ave. , New
   York 10016;   3) Toronto.

Pan Am. Union   Pan American Union (Music Division),
   Washington, D. C.

Paton, Prague.

Paterson's Publications, 36-40 Wigmore St. ,
   London W 1.

Pazdirek, O. , 32 Ceska U 1, Brno.

Peer International (also Southern Music
   Publishing Co), 1619 Broadway, New
   York 10019.

Peters, C. F.   1) Forsthausstrasse 101,
   Frankfurt, a. M. ;   2) Talstrasse 10,

Leipzig;   3) 373 Fourth Ave. , New York
10016.
Pfister
Pinatel, A. , Paris.
Pizzi, Umberto,. 6 Via Zamboni, Bologna 20.
Pleyel, Paris.

Polskie Wyd. Polskie Wydawnictwo Muzyczne.   1) Krasinsk-
Muz.   iego 11, Krakow A 1;   2) Foksal 18,
             Warsaw U 1.

Polyphonic Reproductions, 89 Vicarage Rd. ,
London NW 16.
Presser, Theodore, Bryn Mawr, Penn.
19010.
Pro Art Music Publications, Inc. , 469
Union Ave. , Westbury, L. I. , New York
11590.
Prowse, Keith
Pyraminx Publications, 358 Aldrich Rd. ,
Fairport, New York 14450
Rahter, D. , Werderstrasse 44, Hamburg.
Regia Edition, 28 rue Jean Mermoz,
Paris 8.
Remick Music Corp. (via Music Publishers
Holding Corp.), New York.
Richardson, Norman. , 8 King Edward
Grove, Teddington, Middlesex.
Richault, Charles Simon (now Costallat)
Ricordi   (via Belwin-Mills).   1) Baden;
2) Milan;   3) Paris;   4) New York
Ries & Erler, Charlottenburgstrasse 42,
Grunewald, Berlin.
Riorden, S. , London.
Rongwen, 56 W. 45th St. , New York 10036.

Rouart   Rouart-Lerolle & Cie, 29 rue d'Astorg,
              Paris 8.

Rubank, Inc. , 5544 W. Armstrong Ave. ,
Chicago 60646.
Rubato, Vienna.
Rudall-Carte (now Boosey & Hawkes)
Ruhle, Karl, Heinrichstrasse 11, Leipzig
C 1.
Ruhle and Wendl, Heinrichstrasse 11,
Leipzig C 1.
Russian State (via Musica Rara), Moscow.
Russicher Musikverlag, Berlin.
Sadlo, 233 Kosire, Prague.
*Salabert, Francis, 22 rue Chauchat, Paris 9.

Samfundet	Samfundet Dans Musik, Graadbrødretorv 7, Copenhagen K.
	Sansone Musical Instrument Co. , 1658 Broadway, New York 10019.
	Sansoni, G. C. , Viale Mazzini 46, Florence.
	Saturn Verlag
	Schirmer, George, 3 E. 43rd St. , New York 10017.
	Schlesinger (now R. Lienau), 1) Berlin; 2) Leipzig; 3) Paris.
	Schmidt, C. F. (Cefes Edition), Cacilienstrasse 62, Neckar, Heilbronn.
	Schmidt Co. , Arthur, 120 Boylston St. , Boston 02116.
S	Schneider, Pierre, 61 ave. Raymond Poincare. Paris 16.
	*Schott Sohne, Weihergarten 5, Mainz.
	*Schott. 1) Brussels; 2) 48 Gt. Marlborough St. , London W 1.
	Seeling, Dresden.
	Seesaw Music Corp. , 117 E. 87th St. , New York 10028.
	Selmer Edition, 4 Place Dancourt, Paris 18.
SEMI	Societe d'Editiones Musicales Int. , 5 Lincoln, Paris 8.
	Senart, Maurice and Cie, 20 rue du Dragon, Paris 6.
	Shawnee Press, Delaware Water Gap, Penn. 18327.
	Sieber, G. , Paris.
	Siecle Musical, Edition du (e. Richli), Geneva.
	*Sikorski, Hans, Johnsallee 23, Hamburg 13.
	Simrock, N. (now Lengnick). 1) Bonn; 2) Berlin.
	Simrock, Werderstrasse 44, Hamburg 13.
	Sirene Music (La Sirene Musicale), 29 Blvd. Malesherbes, Paris 9.
	Sirius Verlag, Wiclefstrasse 67, Berlin NW.
Skand. Musfor.	Skandinavisk Musikforlag, Borgergade 2, Copenhagen.
	Ski, Norway.
Soc. Ed. Mus. Int.	Societe d'Editiones Musicales Int. , 5 Lincoln, Paris 8.
Ed. "Science et Arts"	Sophia Edition d'etat "Science et Arts", Sophia.

South. Mus.	Southern Music Co. , 1100 Broadway, San Antonio 78215.
South. Mus. (And. Coll. -22)	Andraud Collection of 22 Woodwind Quintets (via Southern Music Co.), 1100 Broadway, San Antonio 78215.
SMPC	Southern Music Publishing Co. (Peer), 1619 Broadway, New York 10019.
	Soviet Music Center, Moscow.
	Standard
Statni	Statni Nakladatelstvi Krasne Literatury, Prague.
	Stim, Stockholm.
	Templeton Publishing Co. , Inc. , 10 E. 43rd St. , New York 10017.
	Tritone Press (via BMI)
	Ugrino Verlag, Elbchaussee 499a, Hamburg.
	Union Musical Espagnola, Madrid.
Un. Ed.	Universal Edition, Karlsplatz 6, Vienna.
	Universal Edition, Limited, 2 Fareham St. , London W 1.
Univ. Microfilms	University Microfilms, Ann Arbor, Mich. 48100.
Ver. Mus. Wis.	Verlag für Musikalische und Wissenschaft, Hanover.
	Vernede, Versailles.
	Viking Music Press, 34 Nørrebrogade, Copenhagen.
	Weinberger, Jos. 1) 33 Crawford St. , London W 1; 2) Mahlerstrasse 11, Vienna 1; 3) Oederweg 26, Frankfurt, a. M.
	Western International Music. , Inc. , 2859 Holt Ave. , Los Angeles, Calif. 90034.
	Wilder Music, Inc. , 120 Loker St. , Wayland, Mass. 01778.
	Wilke, 17 Hohenzollerndamm, Berlin.
	Witmark & Sons, 488 Madison Ave. , New York 10022.
	Witvogel, G. F. , Amsterdam.
	Wolfe, de, 80-82 Wardour St. , London W 1.
	Wunderhorn Verlag. 1) Kastanienallee 20, Cologne; 2) Munich.
Zen. Val.	Zenemukiado Vallalat, Budapest.
Zen. Arch.	Zentral Archives, Schweizerische Tonkunst, Zurich.
	Zerboni, Suvini, Galleria del Corso 4, Milan.

Zimmerman, Wilhelm. 1) Wohlerstrasse 10,
Frankfort a. M. ;   2) Querstrasse 28,
Leipzig C 1.

*   via Belwin-Mills

OTHER SOURCES

Books, Articles and Catalogues

ACA American Composers Alliance Catalog. New York, 1964.

Alt Altmann, Wilhelm, Kammermusik Katalog. Hofmeister, 1945.

(C) Cobbett, W. W., Cobbett's Cyclopedic Survey of Chamber Music. Oxford University Press, 1963.

(CA) Composers of the Americas (9 vols.). Pan American Union, 1954-1963.

Danzi Repertoire of the Danzi Quintet reported in Donemus Magazine.

Eble Eble Music Co., Iowa City, Iowa.

Eitner Eitner, Robert, Quellen-Lexikon, Academische Druck - U. Verlagsanstalt, 1959. Graz, Austria.

Fetis Fetis, Francois Joseph, Biographie universelle des musiciens et bibliographie generale de la musique. Firmin Didet Freres, 1860-65. Paris.

(G) Gardavsky, Cenek, Contemporary Czechoslavak Composers. Paton, 1965, Prague.

(GR) Robin, Gregory, The Horn. Faber & Faber, 1961, London.

(H) Helm, Sanford, Catalog of Chamber Music for Wind Instruments. National Association of College Wind and Percussion Instructors, 1952. Ann Arbor.

(HO) Houser, Roy, Catalogue of Chamber Music for Wind Instruments. University of Indiana.

23

(J)   Jensen, Richard

(K)   Kirk, Edgar; School of Music, Michigan State
               University.

Lib. Cong.   Library of Congress, Music Division; Washington,
               D. C.

Mc & M   Catalog of Music for Clarinet. McGinnis & Marx,
               1966. Extensive lists.   Unfortunately, publish-
               ers are not noted.

Mc & M   Music for the Flute. McGinnis & Marx, 1968. Ex-
               tensive lists.   Unfortunately, publishers are
               not noted.

(MQ)   Music Quarterly, "Contemporary Music in Europe",
               Vol. 51, No. 1, Jan., 1965. G. Schirmer.

Mus. Ed.   Music Educators Journal. 1201 16th St., NW,
Jour.   Washington, D. C. 20036.

NACWPI   Weerts, Richard, Original Manuscript Music for
               Wind and Percussion Instruments.   Compiled for
               The National Association of College Wind and
               Percussion Instructors, 1962 and 1964.

PP   Pan Pipes. (Sigma Alpha Iota Publication),
               January issues. Sigma Alpha Iota Executive
               Offices, 4119 Rollins Ave., Des Moines, Iowa
               50312.

(R)   Rasmussen, Mary and Mattran, Don, A Teacher's
               Guide to the Literature of Woodwind
               Instruments.

(R)   Rasmussen, Mary, Brass and Woodwind Quarterly.
               Durham, N. H.

(RH)   Ron Hounsell

(S)   Schwann Long Play Record Catalogs.

(V)   Vester, Franz, Flute Repertoire Catalogue. Musica
               Rara, 1967, London.

(W)   Wise, Ron, Scoring in the Neoclassic Woodwind
               Quintets of Hindemith, Fine, Etler and Wilder.

Doctoral Dissertation, University of
Wisconsin, Madison.

(WM)   Woodwind Magazine. Published 1948-1956. Box
            747, Long Beach Island, N. Y.

Colleges and Universities

Alabama State College, Montgomery, Ala. 36104

Ball State University, Muncie, Ind. 47306

Boston University, Boston, Mass. 02215

Bowdoin College, Brunswick, Maine 04011

Cleveland Institute of Music, Cleveland, Ohio 44106

Connecticut, University of, Storrs, Conn. 06268

Conservatorium Cherubini, Florence, Italy

Curtis Institute of Music, 18th and Locust Sts., Philadelphia, Pa. 19103

Drake University, Des Moines, Iowa 50311

East Carolina College, Greenville, N. C. 27834

Eastern Washington State College, Cheney, Wash. 99004

Escola National de Musica, Rio de Janiero, Brazil

Georgia, University of, Athens, Ga. 30601

Hartt College of Music, Hartford, Conn. 06105

Henderson State Teachers College, Arkadelphia, Ark. 71923

Illinois, University of, Urbana, Ill. 61820

Indiana, University of, Bloomington, Ind. 47401

Iowa, University of, Iowa City, Iowa 52240

Michigan, University of, Ann Arbor, Mich. 48106

Michigan State University,   East Lansing, Mich. 48823

New York, State University of, Fredonia, N. Y. 14063

New York, State University of, Potsdam, N. Y. 13676

North Carolina, University of, Chapel Hill, N. C. 27514

North Texas State University, Denton, Tex. 76203

Paris Conservatory of Music (Conservatoire National de
    Musique), 14 rue de Madrid, Paris 8^e

Rochester, University of--Eastman School of Music (Sibley
    Library), Gibbs Street, Rochester, N. Y. 14604

Southern California, University of, Los Angeles, Cal. 90007

Southern Illinois, University of, Carbondale, Ill. 62901

Texas, University of, Austin, Tex. 78712

West Texas State University, Canyon, Tex. 79015

West Virginia, University of, Morgantown, W. Va. 26506

Wisconsin, University of, Madison, Wis. 53706

Wisconsin, University of (Milwaukee), Milwaukee, Wis.
    53201

Libraries

Bibliothèque Nationale, 58 rue de Richelieu, Paris 2^e

Boston Public Library, Boston, Mass. 02101

Elder Library and Conservatory, Adelaide, Australia

Fleischer Music Library, Philadelphia, Pa.

Landesbibliothek, Darmstadt

Library of Congress (Music Division), Washington, D. C.
20540

New York Public Library, Fifth Ave. and 42nd St. , N. Y.
10017

Offentliche Wissenschaftliche Bibliothek, Harburg

Sibley Music Library, Eastman School of Music of Univ.
Rochester, Gibbs Street, Rochester, N. Y. 14604

Other

Adelaide Quintet, Adelaide, Australia

Chicago Symphony, S. Michigan Blvd. , Chicago, Ill. 60605

Danzi Woodwind Quintet, Amsterdam, Holland

New Art Wind Quintet, New York

New York Woodwind Quintet, New York

Woodwind Quintets

ABRANSKY, Alexander (1898-   ).   Concertino. Russian
State, 1929.

ABSIL, Jean (1893-).   Danses Bulgares. Lemoine, 1960;
Mc & M.

_____ .   Quintet.   Mc & M.

ADLER, Samuel.   Intrada for Woodwind Quintet.   Oxford
Univ. Press, 1969.

AGAY, Denes.   Five Easy Dances.   Presser, 1956.

AHRENDT, Karl.   Variegations for Woodwind Quintet.   PP,
Jan. 1969.

AITKEN, Hugh.   Eight Studies.   Elkan-Vogel, 1966.

ALABIEV, Alexander (1787-1851).   Quintet.   Russian State,
1953.

ALBAM, Manny.   Quintet No. 1, 1957.   Lib. of Congress.

ALBISI, A.   Miniature Suite, No. 2.   (HO) Eble.

ALEMANN, Edvardo A.   Serenata, 1960.   Ms. , Lib. of
Congress (Coolidge Found.)

ALJABJEW, A. A.   Quintet.   Sov. Mus. , 1953.

ALLESANDRO, Victor.   Impromptu, 1932.   Lib. of Congress.

AMBROSI, Dante d'.   Introductione e allegro.   Curci, 1963.

AMBROSIUS, Hermann (1897-   ).   Quintet, Op. 57.   Leipzig,
by Composer, 1925.

AMRAM.   Fanfare and Processional.   Mc & M.

ANDERSON, Johannes. Kvintet. Samfundet.

ANDERSON, T. J. , Jr. Five Etudes and a Fancy. ACA.

ANDRAUD, A. (collection). 22 Woodwind Quintets. South.
Mus.

ANDRAUD, Albert J. Quintets of Jongen, Grimm, Leclair
and Liszt. South. Mus.

_____. Sixth Collection (12 Pieces in Quintet Form).
Andraud.

ANDRIESSEN, Hendrik (1892-). Quintet No. 1. Donemus;
Mc & M.
    AA-6. Four movements: Adagio, Vivace, Lento,
    Allegro non troppo. An excellent concert composition.
    Adagio is in 12-tone idiom. All movements are en-
    joyable. Moderate to difficult.

ANDRIESSEN, J. Quintet. Donemus.

ANGELINI, Louis. Quintet. Ms. , (W).

ANGERER, Paul (1927-). Quintet. Doblinger.
    AA-6. Three movements: Adagio-allegro, Largo,
    Vivace. An excellent piece in a conservatively modern
    idiom. Difficult and worth programming.

ANTONINI, Alfredo. Twentieth Century Doll. Chappell,
1968.

ARDEVOL, José (1911-). Quintet, 1957. Ms. , N. Y.
Pub. Lib.

ARNE-COLLINS (arr. Goossens). Suite of Dances. Mc & M

ARNELL, Richard (1917-). Cassation, Op. 45. Peters;
Mc & M.

ARNOLD, Malcolm (1921-). Three Shanties. Paterson's
Pub. , 1954; Mc & M.
    A. Allegro con brio, Allegretto semplice, Allegro
    vivace. Three English work songs dressed in enjoy-
    able, sophisticated settings. The middle song features
    the horn.

ARRIEU, Claude (1930-). Quintette un ut. Noel, 1954;
Mc & M.
    AA-5. I. Allegro; II. Andante; III. Allegro
scherzando; IV. Adagio; V. Allegro vivace. A
valuable piece of a lighter nature, well composed and
enjoyable. Idiom is the early 20th century French
Conservatory similar to Ibert and Francaix.

ASCHAFFENBURG, Walter. Quintet, Op. 16. Lib. Cong.

ASCHENBRENNER, T. (1903-). Quintet. Modern Edition.

ASHTON, Algernon (1859-1937). Quintet. Ms. , (GR).

AVNI, Tzvi. Quintet. Mills, 1966.

AXMAN, Emil (1887-1949). Quintet, 1939. Hud. Mat.

AYRES, Thomas. March. Ms. , Univ. of Iowa.

BAAREN, Kees van (1906-). Quintetto Sovraposizione,
1963. Donemus (Danzi Quintet).

BACEWICZ, Grazyna (1909-). Quintet. Ms. , (R).

BACH, Johann Christian (arr. Maganini) (1735-1782).
Allegretto Piacevole. Fischer.

BACH, Johann Christoph (arr. Maganini) (1642-1703). Allegro
Brilliante. Fischer.

_____. (arr. M. Jones). Sinfonia, No. 1. Presser,
1968.
    B-5. I. Allegro; II. Andante; III. March; IV.
Allegro assai. A rather ordinary, somewhat "bare"
classical work. Like the Rossler quintet, could well
be programmed for historic reasons.

BACH, Johann S. (arr. R. Taylor) (1685-1750).
Kleines Harmonisches Labyrinth. South Mus.
    10 minutes.
Suite in c minor
    15 minutes
Sinfonia in b minor.
    8 minutes
Chorale Prelude, "Christe, du Lamm Gottes"
    2 minutes

Giant Fugue "Wir Glauben All"
5 minutes

_____ . (arr. Maros). Quintetto. Mc & M.

_____ . (arr. Catelinet). Two Fugues from WTC.
Mc & M.

_____ . (arr.   ). Minuet and Haydn Finale. Mc & M.

_____ . (arr. Hirsch). Fugue in E^b. Mc & M.

_____ . (arr. Finney). Sarabande in d (1st French
Suite). B & H.

_____ . (arr. Henschel). Sarabande in d min. Mc & M.

_____ . (arr. Rosenthal). Prelude & Fugue in e min.
Mc & M.

_____ . (arr. Rosenthal). Prelude & Fugue in g min.
Mc & M.

_____ . (arr. Mickens). Bouree. Mc & M.

_____ . (arr. Mickens). Sarabande. Mc & M. B. & H.,
1965.
BADEN, Conrad. Kvintet, 1965. Lib. Cong.

BADINGS, Henk (1907-   ). Quintet No. 1. Donemus,
1929.

_____ . Quintet No. 2. Donemus, 1948.

_____ . Kvintet No. 4. Donemus, 1948.

BAEYENS, August (1895-   ). Quintet. Mc & M.

BAKALEINIKOV, V. (1885-1953). Introduction and Scherzo.
Belwin.

BAKSA, Robert F. Divertimento, 1959. Lib. Cong.

BALAY, Guillaume (1871-1943). Petite Suite Miniature.
Leduc, 1948. Mc & M.

_____ . La Vallee Silencieuse. Buffet Crampon, 1931.

BALCAR, Milan   33

Mc & M.

_____ . L'Aurore sur la Forêt.   Buffet Crampon, 1931.
Mc & M.

_____ . (arr. Waln). Minuet and Rondo.   Mc & M.

_____ . Quintet. Buffet Crampon.

BALCAR, Milan (1886-1954). The Frenštát Idyll, Op. 31,
    1943. (G).

_____ . Dance Suite, Op. 37, 1945. (G).

BALLARD, Louis W. Ritmo Indio. Mus. Ed. Journal
    Feb. 1970

BALLIF, Claude (1924-   ). Quintet, Op. 10.   B & B.

BALLOU, Esther W. Suite. ACA.

BARAB, Symour. Quintet, 1954. Ms. , (J) (W).

BARATI, George (1913-   ). Quintet.   ACA.

BARBER, Samuel (1910-   ) Souvenirs, Op. 31.   Schirmer.

_____ . Summer Music. Schirmer, 1957. Mc & M.
    AA-6. A continuous piece of several moods. Beauti-
    ful and difficult. About ten minutes.

BARBOTEU, Georges. Caricatures. (V).

BARCE, Ramon. Parabola, Op. 22. (MQ).

BARGIEL. Meditations. Mc & M.

BARRAINE, Elsa (1910-   ). Ouvrage de dame.   South.
    Mus. (And. Coll. - 22)
    Theme and variations in a sort of neo-Boulanger style.
    Might be used as·program material.

BARRAUD, Henri. Concertino. Soc. Ed. Mus. Int.

BARROWS, John R. (1913-   ). March. Schirmer, 1950.
    Mc & M.
    A-5. A short, flashy march written in a conservative

20th century idiom.   Ideal for an encore or part of a "modern group."

_____.   Quintet, 1936.   Ms. , Univ. of Wisconsin.

BÁRTA, Lubor (1928-   ).   Divertimento, 1950.   (G).

_____.   Wind Quintet, 1956.   (G).

BARTHE, A.   Aubade.   A. Pinatel.

_____.   Passacaille.   Leduc, 1899; Mc & M. ;   South Mus.
(And. Coll. - 22),
A-5.   An excellent small-scale piece of many pro-
grammatic uses.

BARTOK, Bela (1881-1945).   (arr. R. Taylor).   Gyermek-
eknek.   (HO).

BARTOS, Frantisek (1905-   ).   Le Bourgeois Gentilhomme.
Hud. Mat. , 1934.

_____.   Mestak slechticem.   Hud. Mat. , 1943.
AA-5.   Dance forms in semi-modern settings.   It is
very pleasant music, well worth programming.   The
endurance problems for several instruments are notable.
Piccolo is used in the last movement.

BARTOS, Jan Zdendk (1908-   ).   Quintet, Op. 42. Continental Ed. 1945-46.

_____.   Second Quintet.   (G).

_____.   Third Quintet.   (G).

BARTOVSKÝ, Josef (1884-1964).   Wind Quintet.   (G).

BASS, Eddie.   Woodwind Quintet, No. 1.   ASCAP.

BASSETT, Leslie (1923-   ).   Woodwind Quintet, 1958.
ACA.

BAUMANN, Max (1917-   ).   Kleine Kammermusik.
Sirius.

BAUR, Jurg (1918-   ).   Quintetto Sereno.   Br. & H, 1958;
Mc & M.

AA-6. Six movements: Preamble, Rhapsodia, Scherzo, Spiegel and Krebs, In Memoriam, Finale. A good piece. Suffers from lack of metronome markings which are superseded by vague directions. It is advisable to have a score available. The idiom is a pointal, 12-tone one.

BAUER, Marian (1887-1955). Quintet, Op. 48. ACA; Mc & M.

BAYER-VETESSY, George (1923-   ). Serenade. Modern Ed.

BEACH, B. C. Scherzo. Mc & M.

BEACH, Mrs. H. H. A. (1867-1945). Pastorale. Composers Press, 1942. Mc & M.
A small, bland piece, ineffectively scored.

BECK, Frederick. Two Movements. Ms., (HO).

BECKER, Günther. Serpentinata, 1968. Danzi Quintet.

BEDŘICH, Jan (1932-   ). Wind Quintet, 1956. (G).

BEEKHUIS, Hanna (1889-   ). Elegie en Humoresque. Donemus.

_____. Quintet. Donemus; Mc & M.

BEETHOVEN, Ludwig von (1770-1827). (arr. Vester). Adagio and Allegro fur die Spieluhr. (V)

_____. (arr. Trinkhaus). Adagio and Minuetto. Mc & M.

_____. (arr. DeBueris). Gavotte in F. Fischer; Mc & M.

_____. (arr. DeBueris). Country Dance No. 1. Fischer; Mc & M.

_____. (arr.   ). Country Dance. Fischer.

_____. (arr. DeBueris). Larghetto (and Londonderry Air). Mc & M.

_____ . (arr. van Emmerik). Minuet, Andante and Variations. South. Mus. (And. Coll. - 22).
Very effectively transcribed from a trio. An excellent example of Beethoven's florid variation writing.

_____ . (arr.   ). Quintet from Op. 71. South. Mus. (And. Coll. - 22). Mc & M.

_____ . (arr. Andraud). Variations, Op. 18, No. 5. South. Mus. (And. Coll. - 22).
An excellent transcription, delightful both to play and listen to.

_____ . (arr. Bellison). Variations on "La Ci Davem." Mc & M.

BEGLARIAN, Grant. Woodwind Quintet 1966. Ms., PP. Jan. 1969.

BEHREND, Fritz (1889-   ). Divertimento, Op. 104. Priv. (V).

BELFIORE, Turi. Quintet. (V).

BENGUEREL, Xavier (1931-   ). Successions. Joventuts Musicals, 1962.

BENNETT, David. Rhapsodette. C. Fischer, 1940. Mc & M.

BENNETT, Richard Rodney. Wind Quintet, 1968. Universal Ed.

BENNETT, Robert R. (1894-   ). Dance Scherzo, 1937. Ms., Am. Music Center.

_____ . Toy Symphony, 1928. Ms.

BENSON, Warren. Marche. Shawnee Press.
B-4. (A good encore number. As indicated in the score, the piece has a mood of "comic dignity.")

BENTZON, Jorgen (1897-1948). Suite, Op. 11. Skand. Musfor.

_____ . Racconto No. 5, Op. 46. Mc & M.

BENZON (early 19th Century).   Quintet, Op. 11.   Gombart;
(V).

BEREZOWSKY, Nikolai (1900-1953).   Blas Quintet, No. 1,
1930.   Russian State.

_____.   Suite, Op. 11.   Russicher Musikv., 1936; Mc &
M.

_____.   Suite No. 2, Op. 22.   Mills, 1941; Mc & M.

BERG, Gunnar (1909-   ).   Pour quintette à vent, 1962.
Priv., Copenhagen; Danzi.

BERG, Josef (1927-   ).   Five Fugues for Wind Quintet,
1957.   (G).

BERGER, Jean (1909-   ).   Six Short Pieces.   Zimmerman,
1962. Peters; Mc & M.

BERGMANN, Walter (1902-   ).   Music for Bläserquintett.
Doblinger.

BERGSMA, William (1921-   ).   Concerto.   Galaxy; Mc &
M.

_____.   Two Diversions, 1939.   Ms., (withdrawn).

BERKOWITZ, Leonard.   Quintet, 1966.   Ms., San Fernando
Valley State Coll.
      AA-6.   Time 19:7.   1. ♩ = 132.   2. ♩ = 69; 3. ♪
      = 72; 4. ♪ = 152.   Of moderate appeal.   For ad-
      vanced groups.   It is rhythmically hard, especially the
      last movement.   There is considerable doubling which
      may present problems.   It is a well-constructed, cyc-
      lic, contrapuntal piece.

BERKOWITZ, Sol.   Serenade.   Ms., (HO).

BERLIOZ, Hector (1803-1869).   (arr. R. Taylor).   Serenade
to the Madonna.   South. Mus.

BEVERIDGE, Thomas.   Six Bagatelles, 1964.   Ms., (K),
Mich. State Univ.

BEVERSDORF, Thomas.   Prelude and Fugue.   Ms., Univ.
of Ind.

BEYER, J. M. A Movement for Wind Quintet. Ms., (HO).

_____ . Quintet. Ms. ? (HO).

BEYTHIEN, Kurt. Quintet, Op. 7, 1925. Dresden, by Composer.

BEZANSON, Philip. Homage to Great Americans. Mc & M.

_____ . Quintet. ACA.

BIELSKI, Michael. Quintet. (RH), Univ. of Ill.

BIRTWHISTLE, Harrison (1934-   ). Refrains and Choruses, 1957. Mc & M.

BISSELL. Folk Song Suite. Mc & M.

BITSCH, Marcel (1921-   ). Sonatine for Quintet. Leduc, 1955. Mc & M.
    Three movements: Gaiement, Lent, Moderne. The idiom might be called 20th Century French Conservatory. The piece is enjoyable to play and to listen to. Bitsch uses the instruments well and there are difficult moments both technically and rhythmically for all.

BIZET, Georges (1838-1875). (arr. Williams). Berceuse. Mc & M.

_____ . (arr. Holmes). Minuetto from Second L'Arlesienne. Barnhouse; Fischer

_____ . (arr. Cheyette and Roberts). Minuetto. Mc & M.

_____ . (arr. Cheyette and Roberts). Quintet from "Carmen." Mc & M.

BLACKWOOD, Easley (1933-   ). Quintet. Schirmer.

BLANC, Adolphe. Quintet. Fetis.

BLATNÝ, Pavel (1931-   ). Wind Quintet. 1958. (G).

BLOCK, Waldemar. Serenade. Doblinger.

BLUM, Robert (1900-   ). Concerto, 1961. Zentral Archives.

BLUMENFELD, Harold. Expansions for Woodwind Quintet.
MCA, 1969.

BLUMER, Theodor (1882-   ). Quintet in B^b, Op. 52.
W. Zimmerman, 1924.

_____. Serenade und Thema mit Variationen, Op. 34.
Simrock, 1918.

_____. Schweizer Quintet. Sikorski, 1953; Mc & M.
AA-6. Five movements: Prelude, Gavotte, Arietta
(Fl and Cl), Ruhig (ob), Theme and Variations.
Time--22 mins. An excellent turn of the century work.
The idiom is highly romantic. Requires considerable
technic.

_____. Tanz-Suite, Op. 53. Simrock, 1925.

BOCCHERINI, Luigi. Minuet. Andraud.

BOEDIJN, G. (1893-   ). Quintet Concertante, Op. 150.
Donemus.

BON, Willem Frederik. Quintet. Donemus.

BONGARTZ, H. (1894-   ). Suite No. 11. Ms., (GR).

BONSEL, Adriaan (1918-   ). Quintet No. 1. Donemus;
Mc & M.

_____. Quintet No. 2. de Wolfe, (GR).

BORCH, Gaston (1871-1926). Sunrise on the Mountains.
Belwin.

BORKOVEC, Pavel (1894-   ). Dechovy Kvintet, 1932.
Hud. Mat., 1936

BORODIN, Alexandre (1833-1887). (arr. Hirsch). Chorus
of the Villagers. Presser.

BOROWSKI, Felix (1872-1956). Madrigal to the Moon. Belwin, 1940; Mc & M.

BORRIS, S. (1906-   ). Quintet, Op. 25, No. 2. Sirius.

BOSMANS, Arthur. Diabelliana. H. Elkan, 1957; Mc & M.

BOSTELMAN, Otto. Quintet, 1967. Lib. Cong.

BOTTJE, Will Gay (1925-   ). Quintet No. 1. Ms., Univ. of Southern Ill.

_____ . Quintet, No. 2. ACA.

BOWDEN, Robert C. Quinx, 1967. Lib. Cong.

BOWDER, Jerry. Quintet for Winds. Pyraminx.

_____ . Sonatina I. Lib. Cong.

BOWEN, York (1884-1961). Debutante. de Wolfe.

_____ . Frolic. de Wolfe.

_____ . Berlesque. de Wolfe.

BOZAY, Attila. Quintetto per fiati, Op. 6. EMB; Zen. Val. 1965.
      AA-5. Five movements: Allegro, Lento, Minuetto, Sostenuto, Presto. Good program music in a 12-tone idiom. Not technically hard, but made complex by poor rhythmic notation. No score makes rehearsal difficult.

BOZZA, Eugene (1905-   ). Andante, Op. 48. Leduc; Baron.

_____ . Pentaphonie. Leduc, 1969.

_____ . Scherzo, Op. 48. Leduc, 1944; Mc & M.
      A-6. A dazzling show piece--primarily chromatic. Quite difficult. Its short length makes it first-rate encore material.

_____ . Variations sur un theme libra, Op. 42. Leduc, 1943; Mc & M.
      AA-6. An outstanding modern French program piece, displaying the woodwind quintet effectively in every respect.

BRANT, Henry (1913-   ). Requiem in Summer. ACA; Composers Facsimile Ed. 1956.

BREDOW, Edgar. Frankische Serenade. A. J. Benjamin, 1968.

BREHM, Alvin. Divertimento, 1965. Ms.

BREHME, Hans (1904-). Quintet. (R).

BRENTA, Gaston (1902-). "Le soldat fanfaron."
CeBeDeM, 1956; Mc & M; Elkan.

BRESCIA, Domenico. Dithrambic Suite. Ms., (H).

_____. Second Suite "Rhapsodic," 1922. Ms., Lib.
Cong.

BREUER, K. G. Atonalyse II. Sikorski.

BREVIK, Tor. Divertimento. Ski, 1965. Lib. Cong.

BRICCETTI, Thomas B. (1936-). Three Character
Sketches, 1961. Cont. Mus. Proj.

BRICCIALDI, GIULIO (1818-1881). Quintet, Op. 124. Schott,
1875.

BRIDGE, Frank. Divertimenti. B & H.

BRIGHT, Houston. Quintet for Woodwinds. Ms., West
Texas College, Canyon.

_____. Three Short Dances. Shawnee.

BRITAIN, Radie. A Woodwind Quintet. Robert Brown, PP,
Jan. 1970.

BROD, Henry (1801-1839). (ed. Schuller). Quintet, Op. 3,
No. 1. Mc & M
AA-5. Four Movements: Adagio-allegro, Andante,
Minuetto, Presto. An excellent major work by a con-
temporary of Reicha.

BRONS, Carel. Balletto, 1961. Broude.

BROWN, Charles (1898-). Quintet. Choudens, 1967.

BROWN, Christopher. Divertimento. Gamut, 1965.

BROWN, Newel Kay. Quintet, 1969. Ms., Henderson State
College.

42   The Woodwind Quintet

BROŽ, František (1896-1962). Wind Quintet, 1944. (G).

BRUBECK, Howard. (1916-   ). Quintet. Derry Music Co.

BRUGK, Hans-Melchoir (1909-   ). Serenade, 1959. Sikorski; Mc & M.

BRUNMAYER, Andreas (fl. 1803-   ?). Six Quintets. Fetis.

BRUNS, Victor (1904-   ). Quintet, Op. 16. Hofmeister; Mc & M.

BUCKBOROUGH, James L. Sonatina. Gamble-Hinged, 1938.

BUCZYNSKI, Walter J. Suite, Op. 13. Can. Mus. Cent.

BUECHE. Woodwind Holiday. Bourne.

BULL. (arr. van de Moortel). Prelude and Canzone. Mc & M.

BULL, Edward Hagerup (1922-   ). Marionettes Serieuses, 1963. Lib. Cong.

BUONONCINI. Rondeau (and Schubert scherzo), Op. 166. Mc & M.

BURGHAUSER, Jarmil (1921-   ). Five Wind Quintets. (G).

BURIAN, Emil (1904-1959). Four Pieces for Wind Quintet, 1929. (G).

_____. Variations (on Folk Tunes), 1928. (G.)

_____. Quintet. Alkor Ed.; Mc & M.

BUTT, James. Winsome's Folly, Suite No. 2. Novello, 1960.

BUTTING, Max (1888-   ). Quintet, Op. 30. Ms.? (R).

BYERS, L. J. Suite. Ms., (HO).

CACAVAS, John. Windette. Sam Fox, 1960.

CAGE, John (1912-   ). Music for Instruments, 1938.
   Peters.
      Movement 1: For flute, clarinet, bassoon.
      Movement 2: For oboe, horn.
      Movement 3: Quintet.
      A mediocre quintet. All movements are multimetered.
      The composer has learned to write 8th notes and 8th
      rests at a tempo ♪ = 400.

CAILLIET, Lucien (1891-   ). Concertino. L. Cailliet,
   1956; Mc & M.

_____. Overture in B♭. Elkan-Vogel, 1950; Mc & M.

CALABRO, Louis. Divertimento. Elkan-Vogel, 1966.

CALVERT, Morley. Suite from the Monteregian Hills.
   Can. Mus. Cent.

CAMBINI, Giovanni G. (1746-1825). Quintet, No. 1. Mc &
   M.
      AA-4. Three movements: Allegretto maestoso, Lar-
      getto, Rondo. A rather naive large work of the clas-
      sical period. Cambini's three quintets precede
      Reicha's by 20 years.

_____. Quintet No. 2.

_____. Quintet No. 3. Mc & M.

CAMMAROTA. Introduction, Chromatic Fugue and Finale.
   Mc & M.

CAMPO, Frank P. Five Pieces, Op. 18. Lib. Cong.

CAPLET, Andre (1879-1925). Suite persane. Ms. ? (R).

CARABELLA, Ezio (1891-   ). Suite. Ricordi, 1935.

CARION, Fernand (1908-   ). Fantasie Concertante.
   Brogneaux, 1951; Mc & M.

CARLSTEDT, Jan. Quintet, Op. 19, 1962. Stim.

_____. Symphonia, 1959. Stim.

CARTER, Elliott (1908-   ). Quintet, 1948. AMP, 1955;

Mc & M.

CARWITHEN, Doreen (1922-   ). Quintet. Ms. , (GR),
(V).

CASANOVA, Andre. Four Bagatelles, Op. 11. Priv. ,
Paris, 1955. (V).

CASTEREDE, Jacques (1926-   ). Quintette. Leduc, 1955;
Mc & M.
  Three movements: Allegretto, Andantino, Allegro
  vivace. A light, somewhat sophisticated composition
  that would be effective as a minor piece. Not too difficult.

CASTRO, Washington (1909-   ). Musica de primavera,
1952. Ms. , (CA).

CAZDEN, Norman (1914-   ). Quintet, Op. 96. Lib.
Cong.

_____. Three Constructions, Op. 38, 1941. Kalmus,
1951; Mc & M.

CELLIER, Alexander Eugene (1883-   ). Cinq danses an-
ciennes. Ms. ? (R).

_____. Images médiévales. Ed. Mus. Transatl. 1960.

CEREMUGA, Josef (1930-   ). Wind Quintet, 1964. (G).

CHAGRIN, Francis (1905-   ). Divertimento. Augener,
1952.

CHAILLEY, Jacques (1910-   ). Barcarolle. Leduc,
1948; Mc & M.

_____. Suite du 15th Century. Mc & M.

CHAMINADE, Cecile (arr. Hicks). Scarf Dance. (HO).

CHANDLER, Albert. Valse Emilie. Belwin, 1941. Mc &
M.

CHARPENTIER, Raymond (1880-1960). Quintet. Ms. , (R).

CHAVEZ, Carlos (1899-   ). Soli No. 2, 1963. Mills;
Mc & M.

CHAYNES, Charles. <u>Serenade.</u> Leduc, 1958; Mc & M.

CHEMIN-PETIT, Hans (1902-   ). <u>Quintet, 1947.</u> R.
Lienau, 1949; Mc & M.

_____. <u>Suite, "Dr. Johannes Faust."</u> Peters.

CHEVREUILLE, Raymond. <u>Divertissement, Op. 21.</u>
CeBeDeM, 1962; Mc & M.

_____. <u>Serenade, Op. 65.</u> CeBeDeM, 1960; Mc & M.

CHILDS, Bernard. <u>First Quintet, 1962.</u> ACA.

_____. <u>Second Quintet.</u> ACA.

_____. <u>Third Quintet.</u> ACA.

_____. <u>Fourth Quintet.</u> ACA.

_____. <u>Fifth Quintet.</u>

_____. <u>Take Five (any five).</u> Mc & M.

CHLUBNA, Osvald (1893-   ). <u>Wind Quintet.</u> 1936.   (G).

CHRETIEN, Hedwige. <u>Quintetto.</u> South. Mus. (And. Coll. -
22).
     Two movements: Andante, Allegro con moto.   A light,
     operetta-like pair of pieces.   Not terribly difficult.
     An excellent training piece for this style of music.

CHRIST, William. <u>Quintet.</u> Ms., (HO).

CHRISTENSEN, James (1935-   ). <u>Five for the Fun of It.</u>
Kendor Music; Mc & M.

CICCHESE, David. <u>Toccato, No. 5, 1969.</u> Ms., (RH).

CIESLIK, Kurt. <u>Suite.</u> Lib. Cong.

CIPRA, Milo. <u>Quintet, 1964.</u> Priv. (V).

CLAPP, Philip G. (1888-1954). <u>Prelude and Finale.</u> B &
H, 1941; Mc & M.

CLARKE, Henry Leland (1907-   ). <u>Sarabande for the</u>

Golden Goose. ACA, 1957.

COHEN, Sol B. (1891-   ). Suite No. 1. C. Fischer,
1938; Mc & M.

_____ . Quintet No. 2. Belwin.

COKER, Wilson (1928-   ). Quintet, 1955. Presser, 1964;
Mc & M.
    5. Three movements: Moderate, Slowly, Moderately
    fast. A long piece. First and third movements based
    on restless rhythmic action. Second movement seems
    to be in 3/4 rather than the 6/8 marked. Also its
    ♪ = 56-62 appears to be an exceedingly slow speed for
    both player and listener.

COLACO, Osorio-Swaab, Reine (1889-   ). Suite, 1948.
Donemus.

COLGRASS, Michael (1932-   ). Quintet, 1962. MCA.

COLOMER, B. M. Minuet and Bouree. South. Mus. (And.
Coll. - 22).
    Two very delightful pseudo-baroque movements. Valu-
    able for some programs. Not difficult.

COOKE, Arnold (1906-   ). Quintet. Mills.

COOPER, Paul. Concert for Five. Ms., PP, Jan. 1969.

COPPOLA, Carmine. Quintet. (HO), Ms., 217 77th St.,
Utopia Sta., Flushing, L.I., N.Y.

CORELLI, Arcangelo (1653-1713) (arr.   ) Courante.
Mc & M.

_____ . (arr. L. Taylor). Petite Suite from 18th Century. Mills.

_____ . (arr. Trinkaus). Sarabande and Courante. Kay
& Kay; Franklin.

CORINA, John. Woodwind Quintet. Univ. of Georgia,
NACWPI Bull. Winter, 1968.

CORTÉS, Ramiro. Three Movements for Five Wind Instruments. Ms., PP, Jan. 1969.

COURSEY, Ralph de. Fugue a la Rumba. AMP.

COWELL, Henry (1897-   ). Suite. Mercury, 1949; Mc
& M.

_____ . Ballade. Mc & M.

CRAWFORD, Ruth Seeger (1901-1953). Suite, 1952. Broude.

CROLEY, Randell. Quintet in One Movement. Tritone,
1963; Mc & M.

CROSLEY, Lawrence (1932?-   ). Quintet, 1966. Ms.,
(W).
   AA-6. The composer is Music Director of Cranley
   Films in Ottawa, Canada. This piece is in four movements, but the last two are connected. Its style is
   reminiscent of Bartok, and while difficult, it is a
   worthy composition.

CROUSE, E. A Grecian Ballet. Ms., (HO).

CRUFT, A. (arr.   ). Two English Keyboard Pieces.
Mc & M.

CSONKA, Paul. French Suite for Woodwind Quintet.
Southern-Peer.

CUI, C. (arr. Del Busto). Orientale. Fischer; Mc & M.

CUSTER, Arthur. Two Movements. ACA; General Music,
1968.

DAHL, Ingolf (1912-1970). Allegro and Arioso, 1942. Mc
& M.
   A-6. An excellent 12-tone piece, enjoyable to both
   player and listener. It is one continuous piece approxi-
   mately ten minutes in length.

DAHLOFF, Walter. Der Choral von Leuthen. C. F.
Schmidt 1925.

DAMASE, Jean Michel (1928-   ). (17) Six sept variations,
op. 22. Leduc; Mc & M.

DANZI, Franz (1763-1826). Quintet in B^b, Op. 56 #1.
Mc & M.

_____. Quintet in g min. , Op. 56 #2. Mc & M.

_____. Quintet in e min. , Op. 67 #2, 1824. Mc & M.

_____. Quintet in A, Op. 86 #1. Mc & M.

_____. Quintet in F, Op. 68 #2. Mc & M.

_____. Quintet in d min. , Op. 68, No. 3. Musica Rara.
AA-6. Four movements: Andante-allegretto, Andante,
Minuetto, Finale.
Unusual Danzi with delightful key relationships. At the
tempos assigned would be very difficult.

_____. (arr. Maganini). Gypsy Dance. Mc & M.

DAVID, Gyula (1913-   ). Serenade. Mills, 1960.

_____. Quintet. Zen. Val. , 1955; Mc & M.

_____. Quintet, No. 3. Zen. Val. Gen. Music, 1965.

DAVID, Thomas Chr. (1925-   ). Quintett. Doblinger,
1968.

DAVIDOFF, Sydney E. Pop Goes the Weasel. Ms. , (HO).

DAVIDSON, John. Quintet. (K), Ms. , Mich. State Univ.

DAVIES, Peter Maxwell (1934-   ). Alma Redemptoris
Mater, 1957. Ms. , (C).

DAVISE, Hugo. Danse Suite. Ms. ? (HO).

DeBOURGUIGNON, F. Two Pieces, Op. 71. Mc & M.

DEBUSSY, Claude (1862-1918) (arr. Elkan). Arabesque, No.
1. H. Elkan, 1956; Mc & M.

_____. (arr. Elkan). Arabesque, No. 2. H. Elkan, 1956;
Mc & M.

_____. (arr.   ). Children's Corner Suite. (HO),
New Art Wind Quintet.

_____. (arr.   ). Le Pas sur la neige. (HO), New
Art Quintet.

_____ . (arr. Bozza). Le Petit Negre. Baron; Mc & M.

_____ . (arr.   ). Le Petite Suite. (HO), New Art
Wind Quintet.

_____ . (arr.   ). Romanze. (HO), New Art Wind
Quintet.

_____ . (arr. McGrosso). Suite for Winds. Univ. of
Texas, Dept. of Music.

de COURSEY, Ralph. Fugue a la Rumba. AMP; Mc & M.

DEDRICK, Chris. Sensitivity. Kendor, 1969.

DEDRICK, R. My Baby's Smile. Kendor; Mc & M.

DEFAY. (arr. Wilder). Dance Profane, 1968. Wilder
Pub. Co.

De FILIPPI, Amedeo (Philip Weston, pseud.) (1900-   ).
Arbeau Suite. Concord Music, 1942.

DEFOZZEZ, Rene. (1905-   ). Burlesque, 1928. CeBe-
DeM.

_____ . Quintet. Ms. ? (R).

DEHNERT, M. Festliche Musik. Mc & M.

DEJONCKER, Theo (1894-   ). Quintet. (V).

De JONG, M. Aphoristic Triptique, Op. 82B. Elkan.

DELA, Maurice (1919-   ). Petite Suite Maritime. Can.
Mus. Cent.

DELANEY, Charles. Suite for Woodwind Quintet. South.
Mus. 1963.

DELANEY, Robert M. (1903-1956). Suite for Quintet.
Southern; Mc & M.

DELCROIX, L. (1880-1938). Partita. Ms. ? (GR).

De LONE, Peter. Quintet, 1953. (N), Ms., Wash. State
Univ.

_____ . Quintet, 1957. (N), Ms. , Wash. State Univ.

DELVAUX, Albert (1913-   ). Walliser Suite.   CeBeDeM,
1968; Elkan.

DEMEESTER, L. Divertimento. Mc & M.

DEMUTH, Norman (1898-   ). Pastorale and Scherzo.
Hinrickson.

DENARDIS, Camillo. Allegro Giocoso in E^b.   (HO), Ms. ,
Composer bassoonist at Met.

DENNES, John T. Neo-classic Quintet, 1958.   (N), Ms. ,
1431 Highland Ave. , Louisville, Ky.

de ROOS, R. Incontri. Donemus, 1966.

DESHAYES, Prosper Didier (1820?-   ).   First Quintette.
Gobert (R).

_____ . Second Quintette. Gobert (R).

DESLANDRES, Adolphe Edouard (1840-1911).   Trois pieces
en quintette.   South. Mus. (And. Coll. - 22) Baxter-
Northrup.
    A-5. A very good romantic era quintet. Should find
    a place on a balanced program as there are few
    quintets in this idiom.

DESORMIERE, Roger (1898-   ). (arr.   ) Rameau-
Airs de Ballet. Mc & M.

_____ . (arr.   ). Six Danseries du 16th Century.
Leduc, 1942; Mc & M.
    Scored for English Horn instead of oboe.

DESPORTES, Yvonne (1907-   ). Prelude, Variations and
Finale. M. Baron; Mc & M.
    A-4. A good French composition, worthy of perform-
    ance on any program. Moderately difficult. Excellent
    for young quintet.

_____ . Prelude and Pastorale. Andraud; Mc & M.

DESSERRE, G. T. Suite dans le style ancien. Les Nouvelles, 1956.

DETCHMAN, James Emil   51

DETCHMAN, James Emil (1943-   ). Quintet. Ms., (W).

DIAMOND, David (1915-   ). Quintet, 1957. South. Mus.
  Mc & M.
      BB-5. Three movements: Andante, Theme and Vari-
      ations, Allegro Fugato. A rather dull piece in a 12-
      tone idiom. However, there is compositional correct-
      ness. Moderately difficult.

DIANDA, Hilda (1925-   ). Quintet, 1957. Ms., (CA).

DIEMENTE, Edward. Variations for Woodwind Quintet.
  PP, Jan. 1967.

DIEMER, Emma Lou (1927-   ). Woodwind Quintet, No. 1,
  1962. B & H, 1965; Mc & M.

DIERCKS, John (1927-   ). Quintet, 1955. Presser; Mc
  & M.

DILLON, Robert M. Nocturne and Dance. Ms., (HO).

DIMOV, Bohuslav. Komposition, III, 1968. Danzi.

DITTERSDORF, Ditters. Three Partitas. Br & H.

_____. Partita in D. Musica Rara.

DOBIAS, J. Pastoral. Musica Rara; Mc & M.

DOBIÁŠ, Václav (1909-   ). Pastoral Wind Quintet, 1943.
  (G).

DÖHL, Friedhelm (1936-   ). Klangfiguren. (V).

DOMANSKY, Alfred (1883-   ). Quintet. Schmidt, 1927.

DOMENICO, Olivio di. Quintetto. Leduc, 1955.

DONATO, Anthony (1909-   ). Quintet. Camara.

DOUGLAS, Richard R. (1907-   ). Dance Caricatures,
  1939. Hinrickson, 1950; Peters; Mc & M.

DORAN, Matt. Theme, Variations and Double Fugue, 1951.
  (N), Ms., 4938 Newcastle Ave., Encino, Cal.

DOWNEY, John. Quintet, 1966. Ms., Univ. of Wis. -
   Milwaukee.
      Four movements: A sounding, Assymetrics, Strange
      space, Waveology. A composition based on experi-
      mental tonal and harmonic qualities, with many uncon-
      nected, spastic, rhythmic patterns.

DRAEGER, Walter (1888-   ). Quintet. (V).

DRAGAN, Rafael (1909-   ). Time of Youth. Isr. Mus.
   Pub.

DREJSL, Radim (1923-1953). Spring, Wind Quintet, 1948.
   (G).

DUBOIS, Pierre Max. Fantasia. Leduc, 1956; Mc & M.

duBOIS, Rob (1934-   ). Chants et contrepoints. Donemus.

DUBOIS, Theodore (1837-1924). Passacaille. Heugel.

_____ . Première Suite. Mercury.

_____ . Deuxième Suite. Leduc.

DUNCAN, John. Pastorale, 1956. (N), Ms., Ala. State
   College.

DURAND, Marie Auguste. Rococco Menuet. Schmidt, 1948

DVOŘÁČEK, Jiři. Wind Quintet, 1951. (G). (1928-   ).

DVORAK, Anton (1841-1904). (arr.   ). Humoresque (and
   Hasse Two Dances), Mc& M.
_____ . (arr. Haufrecht). Serenade, Op. 44. ACA.

EBEN, P. Quintet. (V).

EBERHARD, Dennis J. Paraphrases, 1968. Ms., Univ. of
   Illinois.

ECKARTZ, Hubert. Quintet in E^b. Iris.

ECKHARDT-GRAMATTE, S. C. (1902-   ). Quintet.
   Can. Mus. Cent.

EDER, Helmut (1916-   ). Quintet, Op. 25. Doblinger;

Mc & M.
A piece with an interesting variety of 12-tone uses and
supercharged rhythms. Has moments of delight. Technically, moderately difficult.

EDER DE LASTRA, Erich. Blaserquintett. Doblinger, 1968.

EDWARDS, Ross. Quintet No. 1. (V).

_____ . Quintet No. 2. (V).

EFFINGER, Cecil (1914-   ). Quintet, 1947. Ms. ? (R).

EGGE, Klaus (1906-   ). Quintet, Op. 13, 1939. Ms.,
Lib. Cong.

EGIDI, Arthur (1859-1943). Quintet in B^b, Op. 18. Ver.
Mus. Wis. 1937.

EISLER, Hanns (1898-   ). Blaserquintett, Op. 4. Andraud.

EISMA, Will (1929-   ). Quintet, 1955. Donemus.

_____ . Fontamara, 1966. Donemus.

EITLER, Estoban (1913-   ). Quintet, 1945. Ms., (V).

ELGAR, Edward (arr. Trinkaus). Salut d'Amour. Franklin; Andraud.

ELLIOT, Willard. Quintet. Ms., (AR); (Chicago Sym.)

_____ . Two Sketches. (V), Ms., North Texas State
Coll.

EMBORG, J. L. (1876-1957). Quintet, Op. 74. Dania,
1937.

END, Jack. Memo to a Woodwind Quintet. Ms., Sib. Lib.

ENDERS, Anton. Quintet. Mannh. Mus.

ENGELA, Dawid. Divertimento. Ms., (V), 1962.

ENGLERT, Giuseppe Groyo. Rime serie, Op. 5. Donemus.

EPPERT, Carl (1882-   ). Suite Pastorale, Op. 64, 1936.
Ms. ? (J).

_____ . Suite No. 2, Op. 57, 1935. Ms. ? (J).

EPSTEIN, Alvin. Quintet. Ms., Hartt Coll.

ERDLEN, Hermann (1893-   ). Kleine Variationen uber ein
Fruhlingslied, Op. 27, No. 1. W. Zimmerman, 1932.

ESCHER, Rudolph (1912-   ). Quintet, 1967. Donemus.

ESCHPAY, A. Marische Melody. Andraud.

ESCOBAR, Luis Antonio (1925-   ). Quinteto "La Curaba,"
1959. Ms., (CA).

ESSEX, Kenneth (1915-1955). Quintet. Hinrichson; Mc &
M.

ETLER, Alvin (1913-   ). Quintet No. 1, 1955. AMP;
Mc & M.
    AA-6. A major work. Contrapuntal and tonal charac-
    ter is reminiscent of Hindemith. However, the quality
    is a little more pungent.

_____ . Quintet No. 2. AMP; Mc & M.

EVANS, Robert B. Prelude and Fugue, 1967. BMI.
    B-4. Two short movements written with correctness,
    but somewhat dull. Not difficult.

FAIRLIE, Margaret. Woodwind Quintet, 1962. Ms. (V).

_____ . Quintet, No. 3. Priv. (V).

FARBERMAN, Harold. Quintessence. Ms.

FARKAS, Ferenc (1905-   ). Old Hungarian Dances. Zen.
Val, 1959; B & H.

_____ . Serenata. Ed. Musica, 1956; Mc & M.

FARLEY, R. The Night Wind. Ms. ? (HO).

FARNABY, Giles (1565-1640). (arr. Foster). Variations
on Elizabethan Song and Dance Airs. O. U. P., 1957.

FAURE, Gabriel (1845-1924). (arr.). Barcarolle. (HO),
New Art Wind Quintet.

_____. (arr. Williams). Berceuse. Mc & M.

_____. (arr.   ). Les Presents. (HO), New Art Wind
Quintet.

FELCIANO, Richard (1930-). Contractions. Cont. Mus.
Proj.

FELD, Jindrich (1925-). Quintet, 1949. Ms., (V), (G).

_____. Second Quintet. Elder Conservatory.

FELTRE, Alphonse Clarke. Quintets. Fetis.

FENNELLY, Brian. Wind Quintet, 1967. ACA.

FERNANDEZ, Oscar L. Suite, Op. 37. AMP; Mc & M.

FERNSTRÖM, John (1897-). Quintet, Op. 59. Ms. ?
(GR).

FERRARI, Domenico (1780-). (arr. Sabatini). Pastorale. Cor; Mc & M; Camara, 1960.

FIALA, Jiři Julius (1892-). Suite of Czech Dances,
1915. (G).

FINE, Irving (1914-1962). Partita, 1948. B & H, 1951;
Mc & M.
    AA-6. Another major composition of five movements:
    Introduction and Theme, Variations, Interlude, Gigue,
    Coda. Difficult and most effective in its 12-tone idiom.

_____. Romanza. Mills, 1963; Mc & M.
    A-5. A rather strange, introspective piece with many
    musical possibilities.

FINKE, Fidelio (1891-). Quintet. Br & H; Mc & M.

FIORELLO, Dante. Jig and Reels. Ms. ? (HO).

FLAMENT, Edouard (1880-1958). Suite en quintettes Op.
126. Ms., (R).

FLEMING, Robert. Quintet. Can. Mus. Cent.

FLOSMAN, Oldřich. (1925-   ). The First Wind Quintet,
1948. (G).

_____. The Second Wind Quintet, 1962. (G).

FLOTHUIS, Marius (1914-   ). Quintet. Peters.

FOERSTER, Josef Bohuslav (1859-1951). Quintet, Op. 95,
in D, 1909. Hud. Mat., 1925.

FOLPRECHT, Zdened (1900-1961). Quintet, Op. 17, 1938.
Ms. ? (R), (G).

FORET, F. Quintet. Ms., (GR).

FÖRTIG, Peter. Quintet, 1962. Donemus.

FORTNER, W. (1907-   ). Five Bagatellen, 1960. Schott;
Mc & M.

FOSTER, A. Variations by Farnaby. Mc & M.

FOUGSTEDT, Nils Eric (1910-   ). Divertimento in D,
Op. 35b. Ms. ? (R).

FRACKENPOHL, Arthur (1924-   ). Passacaglia and
Fugue, 1953. Ms., State Univ. New York, Potsdam.

FRAGALE, Frank D. (1894-   ). Angora Lake, 1957.
Lib. Cong.

_____. Quintet. AMP, 1948; Mc & M.

FRANCAIX, Jean (1912-   ). Divertissement. Elkan-
Vogel.

_____. Quintette. Schott, 1951; Mc & M.
AA-6. Andante tranquillo; Presto; Thema et variations;
Tempo di marcha francese. A difficult, but delightful
quintet in the early 20th century French Conservatory
idiom.

FRANCL, Jaroslav (1906-   ). Quintetto, 1962. (G).

_____. Reportages, 1963. (G).

FRANCO, Johan (1908-   ). Canticle, 1958. ACA.

_____ . Seven Epigrams. ACA.

FRANGKISER, Carl. Episodes from "Dedication." Belwin.

FRAZIER, Theodore. Quintet. Kendor.

FREED, Isadore (1900-   ). Quintet, 1949. Templeton.

FREEDMAN, Harry (1922-   ). Quintet, 1962. Ms., (CA).

FREY, Emil (1889-1946). Quintet, Op. 47. Ms. ? (R).

FREYER, Joachim. Divertimento. Br & H.

FRICKER, Peter Racine (1920-   ). Quintet, Op. 5.
Schott, 1951; Mc & M.
     AA-6. Four movements: Moderato, Badinerie and
     Musette, Canonic variations, Finale. An interesting,
     but difficult piece. This prize winning composition is
     in a complex, highly contrapuntal and chromatic idiom.

FROMM-MICHAELS, Ilse (1888-   ). Four Puppen, Op. 4.
Ms., (R).

FRUMKER, Linda. Woodwind Quintet, 1966. PP, Jan.
1967.

FURST, P.W. (1926-   ). Bläserquintett, Op. 29. Doblinger.

_____ . Konzertante Musik. Doblinger; Mc & M.

FUSSAN, W. (1912-   ). Quintet. Bar.

FÜSSL, Karl Heinz (1924-   ). Kleine Kammermusik.
Bar, 1943.

FUTTERER, Carl (1873-1927). Quintet, 1922. Kneusslin,
1967.

GABAY, P. Quintet. Mc & M.

GABAYE, Pierre. Quintet, 1959. Leduc, 1961.

GABRIEL-MARIE. Berceuse. Andraud.

GADE, N. W. (arr. Elkan). Merry-Go-Round. Mc & M.

GAGNEBIN, Henri (1886-   ). Quintet. Ms., (J).

GARRIDO-LECCA, Celso. Divertimento for Woodwind
    Quintet. Southern Peer; Pan Am. Union, 1957; Mc & M.
    AA-5. Four movements: Introduction, Variaciones,
    Nocturno, Final-jazz. The composition is mildly dis-
    sonant and rather eclectic, but interesting for the per-
    formers. The last movement seems the weakest. Mod-
    erately difficult technically and ensemble-wise.

GAFER, J. M. (1916-   ). Suite. B & H, 1950; Mc & M.

GEISSLER, F. (1921-   ). Heitere Suite. B & H; Mc & M.

GENTILHOMME. Quintet. Hud. Mat.

GEBAUER, Francois Réné (1773-1844). Quintet I. Hentz;
    Jouve; Sieber.

_____. Quintet II in E^b. Danzi Quintet.

_____. Quintet III. Danzi Quintet.

GENZMER, Harold (1909-   ). Blaser Quintet. Litolff;
    Mc & M.

GEORGE, Thom Ritter. Quintet No. 1, 1966. Lib. Cong.

_____. Quintet No. 2, 1967. Lib. Cong.

GERAEDTS, Jaap (1924-   ). Kleine Watermusick, 1951.
    Donemus.

GERHARD, Roberto (1896-   ). Quintet, 1928. Mills.

GERMAN, Edward. Serenade. Ms.

GERSHWIN, George (1898-1937). (arr. Harris). Promenade.
    Mc & M.

GERSTER, Ottmar (1897-   ). Heitere Music. Schott,
    1938.

GHEDINI, Gioegio Federico (1892-   ). Quintet, 1910.
    Ricordi.

GHEEL, Henry. <u>Waltz in canon on an Irish Lament.</u>   Richardson, 1959.

GHYS. (arr.) <u>Air of Louis XIII and (Schumann, New Year's
Song.)</u> Mc & M.

GIANNINI, Vittorio (1903-   ). <u>Quintet, 1934.</u> Ms.

GIFFELS, Ann. <u>Quintet.</u> Ms. (HO).

GILLIS, Don (1912-   ). <u>Suite No. 1.</u> Mills, 1956.

_____. <u>Suite No. 2.</u> Mills, 1956.

_____. <u>Suite No. 3.</u> Mills.

GILTAY, Berend. <u>Quintetto.</u> Donemus.

GINSBURG, Isaac. <u>Quintet, 1931.</u> Lib. Cong.

GINZBURG, Dov. <u>Fantasy.</u> Israeli Pub. Ag. 1965.

GIRON, Arsenio (1932-   ). <u>Quintet, 1962.</u> Cont. Mus.
Proj.

GLASS, Philip M. (1937-   ). <u>Concertino, 1962-63.</u> Cont.
Mus. Proj.

GLUCK, Christop W. (1714-1787). (arr.) <u>Gavotte.</u> Mc &
M.

GOEB, Roger (1914-   ). <u>Prairie Songs.</u> South. Mus.,
Mc & M.
   Three movements: Evening, Dance, Morning. Clean-
   cut "American" music. Easy, pleasant listening. Moderately easy to play.

_____. <u>Quintet No. 1.</u> ACA; Mc & M.

_____. <u>Quintet No. 2.</u> ACA; Mc & M.

GOLEMINOV, Marin (1908-   ). <u>Quintet.</u> Ed. "Science et
arts," 1954.

_____. <u>Quintet No. 2, 1965.</u> Lib. Cong.

GONZALEZ-ZULETO, Fabio (1920-   ). <u>Suite de Ayer y</u>

de Hoy para Quinteto de Viento, 1956. Ms. , (CA).

_____ . Quinteto Abstracto para instrumentos de Viento, 1960. Southern Peer, 1966.

GOODENOUGH, Forrest (1918-   ). Quintet, 1954. ACA.

GOODMAN, Joseph. Quintet, 1954. Broude.

GÖPFERT, Karl Andreas (1768-1818). Quintets. (V).

GORDON, Ed. (arr.   ). Classics for 3, 4 and 5 Woodwinds. Elkan-Vogel; Mc & M.

GOTTLIEB, Jack (1930-   ). Twilight Crane 1961. Schirmer; Mc & M.

GOULD, Morton. (arr. Taylor). Pavanne. Mc & M.

GOUNOD, Charles F. (1818-1893). (arr.). Funeral March of a Marionette. Mc & M.

GOUVY, L. T. (1819-1898). Serenade. Sikorski.

GRAINGER, Percy A. (1882-1961). Lisbon. Ms. ? (R).

_____ . Walking Tune. Schott, 1912.

GRAM, Peder (1881-1956). Quintet, Op. 31, 1943. Ms. , (R).

GRANDADOS, E. (arr. Elkan). Oriental, Op. 5. Mc & M.

GRANT, W. Parks (1932-   ). Soliloquy and Jubilation. ACA.

GREEN, Ray (1909-   ). Quintet, 1933. Ms. , (R).

GRETRY, A. (arr. Sabatini). Tambourine. Camara; Mc & M.

GRIEG, Edward H. (1843-1907). (arr. R. Taylor). Lyric Suite. South. Mus.

_____ . (arr. Trinkaus). Morning Mood. Mc & M.

GRIMM, Carl Hugo (1890-   ). A Little Serenade, Op. 36.

Andraud, 1937.

GROOT, Hugo de (1914-   ). Burla Ritmica. Broekmans,
1966.

_____. Suite, 1944. Ms., reproduced in Holland.
Voorspet on thema, Siciliano, Habanera, Reel, Blues,
Tarantella. Obtainable in reproduced Ms. form. A
small-scale work in an uncomplicated variation form.
It is neat and delightful to hear, but the idiom is most
conservative.

GUARNIERI, Camargo (1907-   ). Quintet, 1931. Ms. ?
(R).

GUENTHER, R. Rondo. Cundy-Bettoney; Mc & M.

GUENTZEL, Gus. Bas - Bleu. Barnhouse, 1947.

_____. Intermezzo. Pro-Art, 1942.

GUENTZEL, T. Tarantella. Barnhouse.

GUILMONT. (arr. Taylor). Canzonetta. Mc & M.

GUION, D. W. The Harmonica Player. Ms., (HO). In old
Barrare Coll.

GWILT, David. Quintet. Ms., (V).

GYRING, Elizabeth. Fugue in Old Style. ACA.

HAAS, Pavel (1899-1944). Dechovy Kvintet, Op. 10, 1929.
Sadlo, 1934; Mc & M.

HABA, Karel (1898-   ). Quintet, Op. 28, 1945. Ms.,
(R).

HADDAD, Donald (1935-   ). Blues Au Vent. Shawnee,
1966.

_____. Encore "1812." Shawnee, 1966.

HADJIEV, P. (1912-   ). Three Sketches. Bulg. St.,
(GR).

HALL, Pauline (1890-   ). Quintet, 1944. Lyche, 1952.

HAMERIK, Ebbe (1898-1952).   Kvintet.   Dania, 1943; Mc &
M.

HAMMOND, Donald. Quintet.   Ms. , (W), Univ. of Wis.

HANDEL, G. F. (1685-1759).   (arr. Bauer).   Six Little
Fugues.   Baron; Mc & M.

_____ .   (arr. Ross Taylor).   Suite in B^b Major.   South.
Mus.
        AA-4 to 5.   Overture, Sarabande, Gavotte, Minuet,
        Sinfonia.   Excellent arrangements of fine material that
        is technically not too difficult.   Can be used for con-
        cert or training purposes. (15 Mins.)

_____ .   (arr. Boyd).   Suite for Woodwind in C.   Witmark.

HANNAY, Roger.   Divertimento.   Ms. , Univ. of Wis;
NACWPI.
        Four movements: Andante, Scherzando, Moderato grazi-
        oso, Allegro moderato.   "American rhythmic" in nature.
        Has some hard technical spots in all five parts.

HANNIKAINEN, Vaino (1900-   ).   Pastorale, Op. 50. Ms. ,
(R).

HANUS, Jan (1915-   ).   Suite Domestica, Op. 57, 1964.
(G).

HARDER, Paul. O.   Quintet, 1957.   (K), Ms. , Dissert.
Univ. of Iowa.

HARTLEY, Gerald (1921-   ).   Divertissement.   AMP;
1951, Mc & M.

HARTLEY, Walter S.   Two Pieces for Woodwind Quintet.
Mc & M.

HASHAGEN, Klaus (1924-   ).   Rondell, 1964.   Priv.,
Hanover, 1964 (V).

HASSE, Johann Fredrich.   Kammermusik.   AMP; Simrock;
Mc & M.

_____ .   (arr.   ).   Two Dances (and Dvorak Humoresque).   Mc & M.

HAUBIEL, Charles. Five Pieces for Five Winds. Composers Press; C. Fischer; Mc & M.

HAUDEBERT, Lucien (1877-   ). Suite. Senart, 1931.

HAUFRECHT, Herbert (1909-   ). From the Hills. ACA.

_____. A Woodland Serenade, 1955. Rongwen; Mc & M.

HAUG, Hans (1900-   ). Quintet, 1955. Ms. ? (R).

HAWORTH, Frank. Glenrose Suite. Can. Mus. Cent.

HAYDN, Franz Joseph (1732-1809). (arr.) Allegretto
(Symphony II). Barnhouse.

_____. (arr. Philadelphia WW Quintet). Divertimento,
No. I in Bb. Presser.

_____. (arr. Long). Divertimento in C. Schirmer.

_____. (arr. Andraud). Menuet and Presto. South. Mus.
(And. Coll. - 22).

_____. (arr. Frans Vestor). 7 Stücke fur die Flätenuhr,
1793. (V).

_____. (arr. Muth). Quintet (from Klavier trio). South.
Mus. (And. Coll. - 22).

_____. (arr. Reisman). Trio in G. Camara.

HAYS, Robert. Quintet. Ms. , Univ. of Ind.

HEIDEN, Bernhard (1910-   ). Sinfonia, 1949. AMP,
1957.

_____. Woodwind Quintet, 1965. Broude.
AA-6. 1. Variations; 2. Capriccio; 3. Intermezzo;
4. Finale.
Another major modern work in a complex contrapuntal
idiom. Somewhat like Hindemith in organization and
harmonic materials.

HEIM, Max. Quintet in Eb. C. F. Schmidt, 1903.

HEKSTER, Walter. Pentagram, 1961. Donemus.

BB-3.   Five movements: Moderato, Tranquillo, Allegro, Lento. Andantino.
A twelve-tone composition with the wispy quality of Webern. The movements seem quite similar. Technically, not difficult.

_____.   Quintetto a fiato.   Donemus.

HELGER, Lutz.   Cassation.   Dehase, 1963.

HELM, Everett.   Windquintet, 1967.   (V).

HENKEMANS, Hans (1913-   ).   Quintet, 1934.   Donemus;
Mc & M.

_____.   Quintet, No. 2, 1962.   Donemus.

HENZE, Hans Werner (1926-   ).   Quintet, 1952.   Schott,
1953; Mc & M.
   AA.   Three movements: Introduktion, Thema and Variationen; Sehr ruhig; Rasch.
   A sound contemporary composition by an established composer. The problems are rhythmic rather than technical.

HERBERIGS, Robert (1886-   ).   Landelijk Concerto, 1937.
CeBeDeM.

HERMAN, Friedrich.   Quintet.   B & H.

HERRMANN, Hugo (1896-   ).   Kleine Suite, Op. 24a.
Hohner.

_____.   Pastorale Phantasietten, Op. 51.   Simrock; Mc
& M.
   Five short movements: Preamble; Musette; Hirtenchoral; Tanz; Notturno.
   Rather naive music, not too difficult. Would serve young groups very well.

_____.   Romantische Episoden, Op. 13c.   Ms., (R).

HESS, Willy (1906-   ).   Divertimento in B^b, Op. 51.
Hinricksen, 1956; Mc & M.
   Three movements. This piece is quite naive and light in nature. Probably easy to listen to. Good training material.

HEUSSENSTAMM, George. Instabilities. Seesaw Press,
  196?

HEWITT-JONES, Tony. Theme and Variations. Mills,
  1966.

HEYL, Manfred. Quintet, Op. 26. Ms. , (V).

HILLMAN, Karl (1867-   ). Capriccio, Op. 56 (57?).
  Andre, 1923.

HINDEMITH, Paul (1895-1963). Kleine Kammermusic, Op,
  24, No. 2. Schott, 1922; Mc & M.
    AA-6. 1. Playful, moderately fast; 2. Waltz; 3.
    Placid and simple; 4. Rapid; 5. Very lively.
    One of Hindemith's fine compositions. It is considered
    a standard in the repertoire and often played.

HIPMAN, Sylvester (1893-   ). Suite, Op. 11, 1939.
  Artia; B & H.

HIRAO, Kishio (1907-1953). Quintet. Pub. in Tokyo, (V).

HIRNER, Teodor (1910-   ). Wind Quintet, 1960. (G).

HIRSH, Harry. Nocturne. Briegel, 1940.

_____ . (arr.). Turtle Dove. Mc & M.

HIRSCH, Hans Ludwig (1937-   ). Quintetto sereno.
  Peters.

HLOBIL, Emil (1901-   ). Quintet, Op. 20, 1941. Ms. ,
  (R), (V).

HOFFDING, Niels Finn (1899-   ). Kvintet, Op. 35.
  Skand. Musfor. , 1948; Mc & M.

_____ . Kvintet, Op. 36, 1932. Lib. Cong.

_____ . Quintet No. 2, Op. 53, 1953. Pub. by Composer.

HÖFFER, Paul (1895-1949). Variations on a theme of
  Beethoven, 1947. Mitteld. Verl. ; Mc & M.

HOFFER. Blaser Quintet. Eble (HO).

HOFFMAN, Earl A.   Scherzo, 1965.   Lib. Cong.

HOFMANN, Wolfgang.   Serenade.   Sirius.

HOHENSEE, Wolfgang (1927-   ).   Quintet in D.   Br. & H.,
1964; Mc & M.

HOLBROOKE, Josef (1878-   ).   A Miniature Characteris-
tic Suite, Op. 33b.   Bromley, 1904; de Wolfe; Rudall,
1910.

HOLDER, N. H. Derwyn.   Quintet, No. 1, 1963.   Lib. Cong.

HÖLLER, Karl (1907-   ).   Serenade.   Ms. ? (R).

HOLM, Mogens Winkel.   Sonata, Op. 25.   W. Hansen.

HOLMBOE, Vagn (1909-   ).   Nocturno, Op. 19.   Viking
1948.

HOLOUBEK, Ladislav (1913-   ).   Quintet, Op. 20, 1938.
Ms. ? (R), (G).

HOLST, Gustav (1874-1934).   Quintet, Op. 14, 1903.   Ms.,
(R), (V).

HORKY, Karel (1909-   ).   Suite for Quintet, 1943.   Ms. ?
(R), (G).

HOSMER, J. B.   Fugue in C.   Gamble; Mc & M.

HOVHANESS, Alan (1911-   ).   Quintet, Op. 159.   Peters,
1967; Mc & M.
    B-4.   Four movements: Andante, Allegro, Largo,
    Senza misuro.
    Pitch "slides" are part of the composition.   The com-
    position seems dull and uninteresting.

HOVLAND, Egil.   Quintet.   Norsk. , 1968.

HOWARD, Dean C.   Quintet, 1958.   Ms. , (N).

HOWDEN, Bruce.   Three for Five.   Ms. ? (HO).

HOWE, Mary (Carlisle) (1882-   ).   For Four Woodwinds
and French Horn.   Lib. Cong.

HOYER, Karl (1891-1936). Serenade, Op. 29. Simrock, 1924; AMP.

HRUŠKA, Jaromir Ludvík (1910-   ). Wind Quintet, 1950. (G).

HUBER, Klaus (1924-   ). Drei Satze in zwei teilen, 1958. Bar., Mc & M.

HUFFER, Fred K. Divertissement. Witmark, 1934.

_____. Sailor's Hornpipe. Mc & M.

HUFFNAGLE. Candlelight and Crystal. Gornston.

HUGENIN, Charles. Souvenir d'Auvergne. Andraud.

HUGUENIN, Charles. Deux pieces, Op. 21. Leloche; Andraud.

HULA, Zdenek (1901-   ). Four Fairytale Moods, 1941. (G).

HUMMEL, Bertold (1925-   ). Quintet. Simrock; Mc & M.
    AA-5. Three movements: Rubato; Lamentation; Berleske. Possibly a major work. The idiom is enjoyably contemporary.

HUNTER, Eugene. Danse Humoreske. C. Fischer; Mc & M.

HURNIK, Ilja (1922-   ). Quintet, Op. 11, 1944. Ms. ? (R), (V).

_____. Second Quintet, Op. 20, 1949. Ms., (R), (V).

HUSA, Karel. Serenade. (HO).

HUSTON, Scott. Four Conversations for Woodwind Quintet. B & H.

HUYBRECHTS, Albert (1899-1938). Quintet. CeBeDeM; Mc & M.

IBERT, Jaques (1890-1962). Trois pieces breves. Leduc, 1930; Mc & M.

A-5. Three very delightful moods in a light French style. A joy to play and to hear.

ILLÍN, Evžen (1924-   ). Wind Quintet, 1949. (G).

_____ . Children's Suite 1952. (G).

INGENHOVEN, Jan (1876-1951). Quintet, 1912. Wunder-horn. , 1912; Fischer.

IPPISCH, Franz (1883-1953). Quintet, 1926. Ms. ? (R).

ISRAEL-MEYER, Pierre. Quintette á vent, 1964. (V).

IVEY, Jean (Eichelberger). Suite for Woodwind Quintet. NACWPI.

JACOB, Gordon (1895-   ). Quintet. B & H.

_____ . Suite for Woodwind Quintet. (K), Ms. , Mich. State Univ.

JACOBI, Frederick (1891-1952). Scherzo, 1936. C. Fischer, 1938; Mc & M.
A-5. A short, late romantic piece in a conservative early 20th century idiom.

JACOBSON, Maurice (1896-   ). Four Pieces. Curwen, c. 1930.

JACOBY, Hanock (1909-   ). Quintet, 1946. Isr. Mus. Pub. , 1951. Mc & M.

JAMES, Philip (1890-   ). Suite in Four Movements. C. Fischer, 1938; Mc & M.
AA-5. 1. Praeludium; 2. Gavot and Drone; 3. Intro-spection; 4. Fugue & variations.
A good well-composed composition in a conservative idiom with many interesting movements.

JARDANYI, Pal (1920-   ). Fantasie and Variations on a Hungarian Folksong, 1955. Zen. Val. , 1957; Mc & M.

JERSILD, Jörgen (1913-   ). Serenade. W. Hansen, 1951.

_____ . Music-making in the Forest (At Spille i skoven). W. Hansen, 1951; Mc & M.

JETTEL, Rudolf. Quintet. Weinberger.

JEZEK, Jaroslav (1906-1942). Wind Quintet, 1931. Ms. ?
(R), (G).

JIRAK, Karel Boleslav (1891-   ). Quintet, Op. 34, 1928.
Andraud.

JIRKO, Ivan. Quintet, 1949. Ms. ? (RH).

_____. Suita per Quintetto a Fiato. Paton, 1965.

JIROVEC. Cassation. Ms. ? (WM).

JOACHIM, Otto (1910-   ). Divertimento. Can. Mus.
Cent.

JOHNSEN, Hallvard. Serenade, Op. 37. Lib. Cong.

JOHNSON, Clyde Earl (1930-   ). Quintet, 1957 and Overture in C. Univ. Microfilms.

JOHNSON, Eleanor. Legend of Erin. Belwin.

JOHNSON, H. M. Quintet in C. C. Fischer; Mc & M.

JOHNSON, Robert Louis. Suite, 1963. Lib. Cong.

JOHNSTON, Jack R. (1935-   ). Synergism No. 1.
Cont. Mus. Proj.

JOLIVET, Andre (1905-   ). Serenade. Lacour, 1945;
Mc & M.

JONÁK, Zdenék (1917-   ). Wind Quintet, 1964. (G).

JONES, Charles (1900-   ). Five Waltzes, 1948. Ms. ?
(R).

JONES, Kenneth V. (1924-   ). Two Quintets. Ms., (R).

JONES, Tom. Quintet for Woodwinds. Ms., Univ. of Wis.
AA-6. An excellent five movement quintet in a very
compact contrapuntal idiom, tonal but dissonant.

JONES, Wendal S. Wind Quintet, 1960. Ms., Dissertation
Univ. of Iowa.

JONG, Marinus de. Aphoristische Triptiek, Op. 82bis 1953.
CeBeDeM.

_____. Quintet, Op. 81, 1954. Ms. , (R).

JONGEN, Joseph (1873-1953). Concerto, Op. 124, 1942.
Andraud, 1948; Mc & M.

_____. Preambule et danses Op. 98. Andraud, 1937.

_____. Quintet. Mc & M.

_____. Rhapsodie, Op. 70. CeBeDeM, 1922.

JOSEPHS, Wilfred. Wry Rumba, 1967. New Wind Music
Co.
A-5. Wonderfully named--a sophisticated rumba.
About four minutes. Not too difficult technically, but
rather difficult for student groups to achieve total ef-
fect. Good as an encore or part of a group in a program. Might be acceptable at a faster tempo than indicated.

JOSTEN, Werner (1885-). Canzona Seria. Elkan.

JUNGK, Klaus (1916-). Chaconne. Mannh. Musik. ;
Mc & M.

_____. Quintet. Mannh. Musik.

JUON, Paul (1872-1940). Divertimento, Op. 41. Schlesinger (HO).

_____. Quintet, Op. 84. R. Birnbach, 1930.

KADOSA, Pal (1903-). Fuvosotos. Mc & M.

_____. Quintet, Op. 49a. Zen. Val. , 1956; B & H.

KALABIS, Viktor (1923-). Divertimento, 1952. Cesky;
Mc & M.

KALEVE. Quintet, Op. 21. Ms. ? (GR).

KALLSTENIUS, Edvin (1881-). Divertimento, Op. 29.
Ms. ? (R).

KANITZ, Ernest (1894-   ). Quintettino, 1945. Ms. , (N).

KANKAROWITSCH. Aquarelles. Andraud.

KAPP, Villem. Suite. Russian State, 1959.

KARDOŠ, Dezider (1914-   ). Quintet, Op. 6, 1938. (G),
(V).

KARG-ELERT, Siegfried. Quintet, No. 1. Eble (HO).

KARKOFF, Maurice (1927-   ). Quintet, Op. 24, 1957.
For. Sv. Ton.

_____ . Serenade Piccola Op. 34, 1958. For. Sv. Ton.

KARREN, L. Little Tale from Brittany. Andraud.

KASEMETS, Udo (1919-   ). Quintet, 1957. Ms. , (CA).

KAUFFMAN, Leo Justinus (1901-1944). Quintet. Universal
Ed. , 1943.

KAUFFMANN, Fritz (1855-1934). Quintet, Op. 40. Heinrichshofen, 1905.

KAUFMAN, Walter. Partita. Shawnee.

KAYN, Ronald (1933-   ). Inerziali per 5 Esecutori. (V).

KAZDIN, Andrew. Three Movements, 1957. Lib. Cong.

KECKLEY, Gerald. Dances in 4 Rhythms, 1950. Ms. , (N),
Univ. of Wash.

_____ . Quintet. Ms. , (N).

KEETBAAS, Kirk. Quintet. Ms. , (WM).

KEITH, George D. Quintet. B & H, 1948; Mc & M.

KELEMEN, M. Entrances. Peters.

_____ . Etudes contra punctiques. Schott.

KELTERBORN, Rudolf (1931-   ). 7 Bagatellen. Modern
Ed. , 1958; Mc & M.

KELLY, Robert (1916-   ). Passacaglia and Fugue. ACA.

KENNEDY, David E. Wind Quintet in A. Ms., Dissert.,
Univ. of Iowa.

KENNEN, Kent. Quintet. Ms., (HO).

KERN, Frieda. Quintet. Grosch, 1942.

KERN, J. (arr. Harris). Waltz in Swing Time. Mc & M.

KERSTERS, Willem (1921-   ). Quintet. Ms., (V).

KETTERING, Eunice. South of the Border Suite. PP, Jan.
1967.

KETTING, Otto (1935-   ). Quintet, 1968 "A Set of
Pieces." Donemus.

KING, Harold C. (1895-   ). Kwintet, 1940-49. Donemus.

KING, Harold. Quintet in E^b. Peters.

KINGMAN, Daniel. Quintet. Avant, 1964. Mc & M.

KIRBY, Percival R. (1887-   ). Miniature Suite. Ms. ?
(R).

KIRBY, Suzanne Thuot. Elfin Dance. AMP, 1951; Mc & M.

KLEBE, Giselher (1925-   ). Quintet, Op. 3, 1948. Ms.,
(R).

_____. Second Quintet. Priv., (V).

KLEIN, Lothar. Quintet for Winds. Royal Conservatory,
Toronto.
KLEINHEINZ, Franz Xavier (1765-1832). Quintet. (V) re-
ported lost.

KLIMKO, Ronald (1936-   ). Quintet, 1965. Ms., Univ.
of Wis.

_____. A Child's Garden of Weeds, 1964. Ms., Univ.
of Wis.

KLUGHARDT, August Friedrich (1847-1902). Quintet, Op.

79. C. Giessel, 1901; Mc & M.

KLUSÁK, Jan. (1934-   ). Music to the Fountain, 1954.
(G).

_____ . Chess-Playing, 1965. (G).

KNAB. Serenade. Mc & M.

KNIGHT, Morris. Three Mood Pieces. Tritone, 1962; Mc
& M.

KOCH, Frederick. Scherzo for Five Winds. Gen. Mus.
Pub.

KODALY, Zoltan (arr. Elkan). Zongora Muzsika No. 2.
Mc & M.

KOETSIER, Jan. (1911-   ). Divertimento No. 1 Op. 16,
1937. Donemus.

_____ . Divertimento No. 2 Op. 35, 1947. Donemus.

KOHEN, Karl. Little Suite for Wind Quintet. Ms., Mich.
State Univ.

KÖHLER, Wolfgang. Quintet. Priv., (V) Zierenberg.

KOHN, Karl. Little Suite. Priv. (V).

KOHOUT, Josef (1895-1958). 6 Miniaturen, 1946. Mc & M.

_____ . Variationen auf ein Volkslied, 1944. Mann.
Musik.

_____ . Concert Suite, 1937. (G).

KOHOUTEK, C. Quintet. Statni, 1965.

KOHS, Ellis B. Woodwind Quintet. PP, Jan. 1968.

KOLB, Jean Baptiste. Quintets (and trios (ob, cl, bsn)).
Fetis.

KOMMA, Karl Michael (1913-   ). Divertimento, 1955.
Ichthys, 1957.

KONJOVIĆ, Peter. Songe d'une nuit d'eté, 1966. Lib.
Cong.

_____. Suite Concertante, 1966. Lib. Cong.

KONT, Paul (1920-   ). Quintett, 1961. Doblinger, 1963.

KÖPER, Karl-Heinz (1927-   ). Quintet. Priv., (V).

KOPPEL, Herman David (1908-   ). Sonatine, Op. 16,
1932. Skand. Musfor.

KORDA, V. Divertimento. Doblinger, 1965.

KORN, Peter Jona (1922-   ). Prelude and Scherzo. Mercury.

KORTE, Karl (1928-   ). Two Encores, 1961. Cont. Mus.
Proj.

KOSTECK, Gregory. Quintet. Ms. ?, East Carolina Univ.

KOTONSKI, Wlodzimiez. Kwintet. Polskie Wyd. Muz.,
1966.

KÖTSCHAU, Johann (1905-   ). Quintet, Op. 14. Andraud;
Zimmerman.

KOŽELUHA, Lubomír (1918-   ). Wind Quintet, 1962. (G).

KRAEHENBUEHL, David (1923-   ). Canzona, 1953. Ms. ?
(R).

KRAFT, Karl Joseph (1903-   ). Divertimento No. 4, 1943.
Ms. (R).

KRAUSE-GRAUMNITZ, H. Quintet No. 1. AMP; Mc & M.

KREISLER, A. von. Chorale, Prelude and Fugue. Southern SA, 1966.

KREJCI, Iša (1904-   ). Quintet. (V).

KRENEK, Ernst (1900-   ). Alpbachquintet, 1962. (V).

_____. Pentagramm, 1957. Bar.

_____. Woodwind Quintet, 1951.

KRICKA, Jaroslav (1882-   ).. The Wasp. Artia.

_____. Divertimento, Op. 99, 1950. Ms. ? (R).

KROEGER, Karl. Five Short Pieces. Tritone, 1961.

KROL. Eight Pieces. Eble (HO).

KUBIK, Gail (1914-   ). Quintet, 1937. Ms. ? (R).

KUBIZEK, Augustin (1918-   ). Kammerquintett. Doblinger, 1962; Mc & M.

KÜHNEL, Emil. A Little Suite, Op. 29. Grosch, 1942.

KUNAD, Rainer. Musik fur Bläser. Bar.

KUNERT, Kurt (1911-   ). Divertimento No. 2, Op. 18.
Hofmeister, 1956; Mc & M.

_____. Quintet, Op. 4, 1955. Hofmeister.

_____. Quintet, Op. 14. Grosch, 1952.

_____. Quintet, Op. 17. Hofmeister, 1954.

_____. Suite, 1959. Ms. , (V).

KURI-ALDANA, M. Candelaria. Musica Rara.

KÚRTAG, György (1926-   ). Quintet, Op. 2, 1959. Zen.
Val. , 1965.

KVAPIL, Jaroslav (1892-1961). Quintet, 1935. Ms. ? (R),
(V), (G).

LABATE, Bruno. Intermezzo, No. 2. Mills, 1954.

LABEY, Marcel (1875-   ). Quintet. Rouart, 1923.

LACERDA, Osvaldo (1927-   ). Variations & Fugue.
Peer, 1965.

LACHNER, Franz (1803-1890). Quintet in F, 1823. Ms. ,
(R).

_____ . Quintet in E^b, 1829. Ms., (R).

LADERMAN, Ezra (1924-   ). Quintet. ACA.

LAKS, Szymon (1901-   ). Quintet, 1929. Ms. ? (R).

LANDAU, Victor. Partita. ACA.

LANDRE, Guillaume (1905-   ). Blaaskwintet, 1930.
Donemus.

_____ . Quintet, 1960. Donemus.

LANG, Istvan. Quintetto, 1965. Zen. Val., 1965.

_____ . Quintet No. 2, 1967. Zen. Val.

LANGE, Hans (1882-   ). Böhmische Musikanten, Op. 40.
Berlin, The Composer, 1938.

_____ . Quintet, Op. 14. Berlin, The Composer, 193?

LARSEN, E. Three Morceau. Schott.

LASSEN, Robert. Quintet, Op. 3, 1965. Lib. Cong.

LAUDENSLAGER, Harold. Quintet. Cor.

LAURISCHKUS, Max (1876-1929). Aus Litauen, Suite, Op.
23. Simrock, 1914.

LAVENDER, William Davis (1921-   ). Divertimento.
Lib. Cong.

LAWSON, Robert D. Woodwind Quintet. Fairport, N.Y.,
Mus. Ed. Jour. Feb. 1970.

LAZAROF, Henri. Concertino da Camera. Irs. Mus. Pub.,
1965.

LECLAIR, Jean Marie. Three Petité Pieces de Concert.
Andraud.

LEDUC, Jacques. Quintet, 1960. Maurer, 1960.

LEEUW, Ton de. Antifonie for Wind Quintet and 4 Sound
Tracks. Donemus.

LEFEBVRE, Charles Edouard (1843-1917).   (arr. Waln).
Prelude from 2nd Suite, Op. 122.   Kjos.

_____ .   Quintet, Op. 57, or Suite, Op. 57.   Hamelle,
1910 South. Mus. (And. Coll. - 22); Mc & M.
AA-5.   Very effective romantic "French" style music.
Individual movements, especially the last, are also
good when played alone.   This feature makes this a
valuable composition.

LEGLEY, V. Quintet, Op. 58.   Mc & M.

LEHMANN, Hans Ulrich (1937-   ).   Episoden, 1963.   Ars
Viva, 1965.

LEIBOWITZ, Rene (1913-   ).   Quintette a vent.   Bomart,
1958.

LEICHTLING, Alan. Quintet, No. 3.   Seesaw Press.

LENDRAI, Erwin (1882-1949).   Quintet, Op. 23.   Simrock,
1922.

LESSARD, John (1920-   ).   Partita.   Joshua Corp.

LEUKAUF, Robert (1902-   ).   Quintet, Op. 25.   Doblinger, 1965; Mc & M.

LEVY, F. (arr. Riebold).   Lovelette.   Belwin.

LEWIN, G. Quintet.   Andraud, (HO).

LEWIS, Peter T.   Contrasts.   ACA.

_____ .   Five Movements.   ACA.

LHOTKA, Fran (1883-   ).   Pastoral and Scherzo, 1949.
Ms. ? (R).

LICKL, Johann Georg (1769-1843).   Quintetto Concertante.
Haslinger Kneusslin, 1966.

LIGETI, György (1923-   ).   Five Bagatelles.   (withdrawn).

LILGE, Hermann.   Variationen und Fuge uber ein eigenes
Thema, Op. 67.   Kistner & Siegel, 1937.

LILIEN, Ignace (1897-   ). Quintetto II, 1952. Donemus.

_____ . Voyage au printemps, 1950. Donemus.

LINDER, H. (1795-1846). Quintet, Op. 1. Hofmeister.

LINDNER, Franz or Friedrich (1795-1846). Quintet, No. 1.
Hofmeister, Fetis.

LINDPAINTER, Peter Josef. Symphonie Concertante, Op. 4.
Schott.

_____ . Symphonie Concertante, Op. 36. Schott.

LINN, Robert. Woodwind Quintet. Avant.

LIST, Kurt. Quintet. Ms. ? (HO).

LISZT, Franz (1811-1886). (arr. Hamilton). Pastorale from
"Les Preludes." Galaxy.

_____ . (arr. Seay). Weihnachslied. Mc & M.

LOBODA, Samuel R. (1916-   ). Suite in Introspect 1952.
Lib. Cong.

LOCKWOOD, Norman (1906-   ).   Fun Piece for Woodwind
Quintet. PP, Jan. 1967.

LOHSE. Quintett. Peters.

LONDON, Edwin. Quintet, 1960. Lib. Cong.

LONGAZO, George. Quintet. (HO), Ms., Univ. of Ind.

LORA, Antonio (1899-   ). Quintet. ACA.

_____ . Six Dances, Old and New. Mc & M.

LORENZO, Fernandez, Oscar (1897-1948). Suite, Op. 37,
No. 2, 1926. AMP, 1942.

LOUEL, Jean (1914-   ). Quintet, 1958. Mc & M.

LUCKHARDT, Hilmar (1913-   ). Woodwind Quintet No. 1,
1966. Ms., Univ. of Wis.
    AA-5. One of the outstanding pieces in the quintet

repertoire. Well-written in every respect and a delight to play and to hear. Four movements with the
last two connected.

LUCKY, Stepan. (1919-   ). Quintet, Op. 2, 1946. (R).

LUENING, Otto (1900-   ). Fuguing Tune. AMP, 1944.

LUNDEN, Lennart (1914-   ). Rondino. Norsk.

_____. Variations on Byssan Lull. Chester; Mc & M.

LUTYENS, Elizabeth (1906-   ). Quintet, 1960. Ms., (C).

McBRIDE, Robert (1911-   ). Five Winds Blowing, 1957.
ACA.

_____. Home on the Range. ACA.

_____. Rock 'Em Cowboy. ACA.

_____. Quatro Milpas. ACA.

_____. Mexican Dance. ACA.

_____. Serenade to Country Music. ACA.

_____. Jam Session, 1941. Composers, 1944; Mc & M.

McCALL, H. E. Two Tunes from Mother Goose. Andraud,
Mc & M.

McCOLLIN, Frances (1892-   ). Diversion for Five Instruments, 1943. Ms., (R).

MacDONALD, Malcolm (1916-   ). Divertimento. Ms.,
(GR).

MacDOWELL, Edward (1861-1908). (arr. Trinkaus). Idyl,
Op. 28, No. 2. Mc & M.

McEWEN, John B. Under Northern Skies, 1939. Ms., (GR).

McINTYRE, Paul. Fantasy on an Eskimo Song. Can. Mus.
Cent.

McKAY, George F. (1899-   ). Three Nautical Characters.

Barnhouse, 1954.

_____ . Joyful Dance.   Mercury, 1949.

_____ . Quintet, 1930.   Ms. , (R).

McKINLEY, Carl (1895-   ).   Suite for Five Instruments.
Ms. , (R).

McLAUGHLIN.   Six Fragments for Woodwind Quintet.   PP,
Jan. 1968.

McPEEK, Benjamin.   Quintet.   Can. Mus. Cent.

MACERO, Teo.   Pieces for Children.   ACA.

MAEGAARD, Jan.   Quintet.   Ms. ? (R).

MAGANINI, Quinto.   Fox Trot Burlesque on "Simple Aveu."
C. Fischer, 1932; Mc & M.

_____ . (arr. Harris).   Reverie.   Andraud.

MÄGI, S.   Ostinato.   Russ. St. , 1965.

MAHOUD, Parviz.   Quintet.   Ms. , (HO).

MAILMAN, Martin.   Woodwind Quintet.   PP, Jan. 1969.

MALIPIERO, Gian Francesco (1882-   ).   Dialoghi IV, 1956.
Ricordi, 1957; Mc & M.

MALIPIERO, Riccardo (1914-   ).   Musica da Camera.   Mc
& M.

_____ . Quintet, 1959.   Zerboni.

MALOVEC, Jozef (1933-   ).   Cassation.   (G).

MAMIYA, Michio (1929-   ).   Three Movements.   Lib.
Cong. ; Pub. in Tokyo, 1963.

MAMLOK, Ursula.   Quintet for Wind Instruments.   ACA.

MANDIC, Joseph (1883-   ).   Quintet.   Universal Ed. , 1933.

MANEVICH, Aleksandr.   Quintet.   Leeds, 1959.

MANGOLD, Wilhelm   81

MANGOLD, Wilhelm (1796-1875). Quintet. Schott; Fetis.

MANIET, R. Quintet. Maurer.

MARAGNO, Virtu. Divertimento, 1952. Ms. , (CA).

MARCKHL, Erich. Sonata. Doblinger, 1968.

MARECHAL, Henri-Charles. (1842-1924). Air du guet.
Heugel, 1920; Mc & M.

_____ . Night Watch Tune of King Rene. Andraud.

MAREZ, Oyens, Tera de. Two Sketches. Donemus, 1963.

MARIC, Ljubica (1909-   ). Quintet, 1933. Ms. ? (R).

MARIE, Gabriel (arr. Harris). Berceuse. Cundy-Bettoney.

MAROS, Rudolph. (1917-   ). Musica Leggiera 1956.
Zen. Val. , 1958; Ed. Musica, 1958; Mc & M.

MARTELLI, Henry (1895-   ). Quintet, No. 1, 1948. Ms. ,
(R).

MARTIN, Carroll. Prestissimo. B & H, 1940.

MARTIN, Frank. Prestissimo. Belwin, 1940; Mc & M.

MARTINO, Donald. Concerto. Ms. , (W) (rental-Mc & M).

MARTINON, Jean (1910-   ). Quintet, 1938. Ms.

MARTINU, Bohuslav (1890-1959). Quintet, 1930. Chester.

MARUTA, Shozo (1928-   ). Divertissement. Lib. Cong. ;
Pub. Tokyo, 1965.

MARVIA, Einari (1915-   ). Quintet, Op. 8. Ms. ? (R).

MASON, Daniel Gregory (1873-1953). Divertimento, Op. 26b,
1927. Witmark, 1936; Mc & M.

MASSON, Paul-Marie (1882-1954). Suite Pastorale. Ms. ?
(R).

MAŠTALÍŘ, Jaroslav (1906-   ). Wind Quintet, No. 1,
1933. (G).

_____ . Wind Quintet, No. 2, 1941. (G).

_____ . Wind Quintet, No. 3, 1943. (G).

MATARAZZO, J. Quintet. Camara.

MATTHEW, D. (1919-   ). Partita. Ms. , (GR).

MATTIE-KLICKMAN. Victoria Gavotte in A^b. Standard
(HO).

MATYS, Jiři (1927-   ). Wind Quintet, Op. 10, 1951. (G).

MAY, Walter A. Quintet. Priv. , Cincinnati, O. 1965.

MEDERACKE, Kurt. Böhmische Suite, Op. 43. Hofmeister,
1948; Mc & M.

MEEK, Charles. Slumber Suite. Ms. ? (HO).

MEESTER, Louis de (1904-   ). Divertimento, 1946.
CeBeDeM.

MELLIN, G. Menuet Badin. Andraud.

MENDELSOHN, Alfred (1910-   ). Sapte Miniaturi. Lib.
Cong. ; Editura Muzicala, 1963.

MENDELSOHN, J. Arko. Figurate Hymn. Fischer, 1939.

MENDELSSOHN, Felix (1809-1847). (arr. R. Taylor).
Kinderstucke. South. Mus.

_____ . (arr. Seay). Scherzetto, Op. 102, No. 3. Mc
& M.

MENGAL, Martin Joseph (1784-1851). Three Quintets.
Pleyel, Fetis.

MENGELBERG, Misja. Omrent een Componisten-actie.
Donemus.

MERSSEN, Boris. Musik fur Blaserquintett. Br. & H,
1968.

MEULEMANS, Arthur (1884-   ). Quintet No. 1. CeBe-
DeM, 1957; Mc & M.

_____ . Quintet No. 2. CeBeDeM, 1957; Mc & M.

_____ . Quintet No. 3. CeBeDeM, 1961; Mc & M.

MEYER-TORMIN, Wolfgang (1911-   ). Kleines Quintett.
B & B, 1964; Mc & M.

MEYEROWITZ, Jan. (1913-   ). Quintet, 1954. Rongwen.

MIAGI, Ester Kustovna. Ostinato. Russ. St. , 1964.

MICHEELSEN, Hans Friedrich (1902-   ). Divertimento.
(V).

_____ . Ei, du feiner Reiter. Bar. , 1957.

MIGOT, Georges (1891-   ). Quintette. Leduc, 1955;
Mc & M.

MIHULE, Jiři (1907-   ). Wind Quintet, 1945. (G).

MIKODA, Bořivoj (1904-   ). Wind Quintet, 1948? (G).

MILHAUD, Darius (1892-   ). Divertissement. Huegel,
1958; Mc & M.
     BB-4. Seems to be average Milhaud. The three
     movements are longer than those of "The Cheminee"
     but, except for the third, do not appear as interesting.

_____ . La Cheminee du roi Rene, 1939. Andraud, 1942;
Mc & M.
     AA-5. Seven movements in a delightfully modern
     pseudo-rustic idiom. This is a standard piece in the
     quintet repertoire with interest for all.

_____ . Two Sketches. Mercury, 1946.
     A-4. 1. Madrigal; 2. Pastoral.
     These two pieces are similar to two of the movements
     in "The Cheminee," but somewhat more developed.
     Both are delightful and can be used in many ways in a
     program.

MILLER, John Lewis. Five Fragments. Pyraminx.

MILLER, Kenneth B. Ode to Spring. Byron Douglas Pub.;
Lib. Cong., 1966.

MILLER, Lewis M. (1933-   ). Sonatina, 1961-62. Cont.
Mus Proj.; Univ. Micro.

MILLER, Ralph Dale. Three American Dances. Fischer.

MILLS, Charles (1914-   ). Chamber Concertante Op. 17,
1941. Ms.? (R).

_____ . Sonata Fantasia. ACA.

MILNER, Anthony. Quintet. Univ. Ed., 1964.

MIRANDOLLE, Ludovicus (1904-   ). Deux morceau, II.
La Haye, by Composer, 1952.

MLEJNEK, Vilém Prokop (1906-   ). Wind Quintet, 1959.
(G).

_____ . Wind Quintet, 1962. (G).

MOESCHINGER, A. (1897-   ). Quintet. Ms. ? (GR).

MOHR, Wilhelm (1904-   ). Quintet, Op. 6, 1943. Ms.,
(V).

_____ . Variationen uber das Lied von Henschreck. Kasparek.

MOLNAR, Antol. (1890-   ). Quintet, Op. 16. Ms., (R).

MONACO, Richard. Quintet. Ms., (W).

MONDELLO, H. (Toots). Quintet. Ms., (W).

MOORE, Charles (1938-   ). Quintet, 1964. Mills, 1966.

MOORE, Douglas (1893-   ). Quintet, 1942. Schirmer,
1948; Mc & M.

MORITZ, Edvard (1891-   ). Quintet, Op. 41. South. Mus.
(And-Coll. - 22); Zimmerman, 1928.
    Allegro; Scherzo; Andante; Finale.
    A naive composition of the romantic period. Question-
    able program material.

MORRIS, Franklin E. (1920-   ). Five Esoteric Pieces.
Ms. ? (S).

MORSE, Richard W. The Griesinger Suite. Ms. , Sibley
Lib.

MORTARI, Virgilio (1902-   ). Petite offrande Musicale.
Leduc.

MORTEL, L. van de. Preludio e canzoni. Mc & M; (V).

_____ . Kings Hunting Jib. Mc & M; (V).

_____ . John Bull. Mc & M; (V).

MORTENSEN, Finn (1922-   ). Quintet, Op. 4. Hansen,
1957.

MORTENSEN, Otto (1907-   ). Quintet. Hansen; Mc & M.

MOTTE, Diether de la (1928-   ). Quintet, 1954. The
Composer, 1954.

MOULAERT, Pierre. Passepied en Rondo. CeBeDeM, 1968.

MOULAERT, Raymond (1875-   ). Concerto. Ms. , Lib.
Cong.

MOUSSORGSKY, M. (1839-1881). (arr. Kessler). Ballet of
the Unhatched Chicks. Mc & M.

MOYSE, L. Quintet. Mc & M.

MOYZES, Alexander (1906-   ). Quintet, Op. 17. Simrock, 1943.

MOYZES, Mikulas (1872-1944). Quintet. Ms. , (R).

MOZART, Wolfgang A. (1756-1791). (arr. R. Taylor).
Adagio and Allegro "Ein Stuck fur ein Orgelwerk in eine
"Uhr." South. Mus.

_____ . (arr. Weigelt). Adagio in B^b, K. 411. Mc & M.

_____ . (arr.   ). Adagio. Mc & M.

_____ . (arr. Calliet). Allegro Concertante. Mc & M.

_____ . (arr. Meyer). Andante in F, K. 616. Mc & M.

_____ . (arr.   ). Divertimento No. 2. Mills.

_____ . (arr. Weigelt). Divertimento No. 8, K. 213.
Mc & M.

_____ . (arr. Weigelt). Divertimento No. 9, K. 240.
Mc & M.

_____ . (arr. Weigelt). Divertimento No. 13, K. 253.
Mc & M.

_____ . (arr. Weigelt; also Van de Moortel; Baines).
Divertimento No. 14, K. 270. Mc & M.

_____ . (arr. Meyer). Fantasie K. 608. Mc & M.

_____ . (arr. Meyer). Fantasie K. 594. Mc & M.

_____ . (arr. Waln). Menuet. Mc & M.

_____ . (arr. Andraud). Minuet and German Dance.
South. Mus. (And. Coll. - 22).

_____ . (arr. Calliet). Quintet from Oboe Quartet. Mc
& M.

_____ . (arr. Snieckowski). Trio, K. 422. Mc & M.

MUCZYNSKI, Robert (1929-   ). Movements, Op. 16, 1962.
Shawnee.

MUELLER, Frederick. Five Pieces for Quintet. Cor; Mc
& M.

_____ . Three Transcriptions. Mc & M.

MUELLER, Peter (see Müller).

MUFFAT, Georg (ed. Woehl). Suite aus dem Blumenbusch-
lein. Bar.

MULDER, Hermann (1894-   ). Quintet, Op. 119. Donemus.

MULLER, F. Three Transcriptions. Camara.

MÜLLER, Peter (1791-1877). Quintet No. 1 in E^b. Ruhle,
1874; Musica Rara; Mc & M.

_____ . Quintet No. 2. Musica Rara.

_____ . Quintet No. 3. Musica Rara.

MÜLLER-RUDOLSTADT, Willy. Die Leineweber. Grosch,
1933.

MULLER VON KULM, Walter (1899-   ). Triptychon, Op.
85. Lib. Cong.

MURRAY, Bain (1926-   ). Quintet, 1963. Ms. , (W).

MYERS, Robert (1941-   ). Two Movements. Cont. Mus.
Proj.

NECKE. Mills of San-Souci. Mills.

NEJEDLÝ, Vit (1912-1945). Two Compositions for Wind
Quintet, Op. 8a, 1934. (G).

NELHYBEL, Vaclav (1919-   ). Quintet, No. 1, 1949.
Eulenberg, 1954.

NERO, P. Monsoon in B^b. C. Fischer; Mc & M.

NEVIN, Ethelbert W. (arr. P. Gordon). Gondolieri.
Presser; Mc & M.

NIELSEN, Carl (1865-1931). Kvintet, Op. 43. Hansen; 1923
Mc & M.
    AA-6. A great composition for woodwind quintet. The
    style is a conservative neo-romantic one. English horn
    is used in the third movement. In the last movement,
    "A theme and variations," each instrument is shown in
    solo to great advantage.

NILSSON, Bo (1937-   ). Zwanzig Gruppen, 1958. Ms. ?

NOHR, Christian Frederich (c. 1800-   ). Pot-pourri, Op.
3. Br. & H.

NORMAND, Albert. Quintette, Op. 45. Vernede, 1890?
South. Mus. (And. Coll. - 22)
    A very poor piece, naive and requiring a minimum

of technique.

NORTH, Alex (1910-   ).   Quintet, 1942.   Ms. , (R).

NOVAK, Jan (1921-   ).   Concertino.   Hud. Mat. , 1959.

NOWKA, Dieter (1924-   ).   Quintet, 1955.   (V).

NYBERG, Gary (1945-   ).   Wind Quintet No. 1.   Ms. ,
Univ. of Wis.

NYMAN, Uno (1879-   ).   Arctic Suite, 1934.   Ms. , (R).

OBERSTADT, Carolus D. (1871-1940).   Quintet.   Ms. ? (C).

OBRECHT, Eldon.   Pantomimes.   Ms. , Univ. of Iowa.

O'FARRILL, A.   Quintet.   Ms. , (W).

OLSEN, Sparre (1903-   ).   Quintet, Op. 35.   Peters;
Lyche, 1950; Mc & M.

O'MEAGHER, Hugh.   Woodwind Quintet, 1963.   Lib. Cong.

ONSLOW, George (1784-1853) (ed. Redel).   Quintet, Op. 81
No. 1, 1852.   Leuckhart, 1956; Kistner; Mc & M.

_____ .   (ed. Redel).   Quintet, Op. 81 No. 2, 1852.
Leuckhart, 1956; Kistner; Mc & M.

_____ .   (ed. Redel).   Quintet, Op. 81 No. 3, 1852.
Leuckhart, 1956; Kistner; Mc & M.
AA-5. (F Major).   1. Allegro non troppo;   2. Scherzo;
3. Andante sostenuto;   4. Finale, Allegro spirituoso.

ORLANDO, Michele (1887-   ).   Interludio Sinfonico.   (R).

_____ .   Quintet, Suite.   (R).

OSSINSKY, Louis (1931-   ).   Suite, 1955.   Lib. Cong.

OSTERC, Slavko (1895-1941).   Quintet, 1932.   (R).

OTS, K.   Pieces for Wind Quintet.   Russ. St.

OTSA, Harry.   Quintet.   Ms. , Univ. of Wis.
The composer is a contemporary Esthonian, if there is

such a thing. The work is less than ordinary musi-
cally and of medium difficulty. Presently unavailable.

OTTEN, Ludwig (1924-   ).   Blaasquintet II, 1954.   Donemus.

_____ .   Movements for Wind Quintet (Blaaskwintet No. 3),
1966. Donemus.

OTTOSSON, David (1892-   ).   Suite.   (R).

OUBRADOUS, Fernand (1903-   ).   Fantaisie Dialoguee.
Oiseaulyre, 1949.

_____ .   Symphonies et Danses.   Leduc; 1954.

OWEN, Blythe.   Two Inventions for Woodwind Quintet.   PP,
Jan. 1968.

PACIORKIEWICZ, Tadeusz.   Quintet, 1951.   Po. Wyd. Muz.

PALKOVSKÝ, Oldřich (1907-   ).   Wind Quintet No. 1, Op.
21, 1949.   (G).

_____ .   Wind Quintet No. 2, 1958.   (G).

PALMER, Robert (1915-   ).   Quintet, 1951.   Ms. ? (W)
Cornell Univ.

PANBENI, G. C. (1881-   ).   Suite in Tre Tempi.   Ms. ?
(GR).

PANUFNIK, Andrzej (1914-   ).   Quintet, 1953.   Po Wyd.
Muz.

PAPINEAU-COUTRE, Jean (1916-   ).   Fantasie pour
Quintet.   BMI.

PARKS, W. Grant.   Soliloquy and Jubilation for Woodwind
Quintet.   PP, Jan. 1967.

PARRIS, Herman.   Miniatures.   H. Elkan, 1956; Mc & M.
Not very exciting music, but it is relatively easy.   The
texture seems much the same in most of the fifteen
small movements.

PARRIS, Robert (1924-   ).   Sonatina.   ACA.

_____ . Five Easy Canons and a Fugue. ACA.

PARROT, Ian (1916-   ). Quintet, 1948. Ms., (V).

PARTOS, Oedoen (1907-   ). Quintet. Isr. Mus. Inst.,
    1966.

PARTOS, Oedon. Nebulae. (V).

PASSANI, E. Quintette. Mc & M.

PATTERSON, Aandy. Suite, 1962. Ms., (N).

PATTERSON, Paul (1947-   ). Wind Quintet. Weinberger,
    1968.

PAUER, Jiri (1919-   ). Dechový Kvintet, 1963. Statni.
    Hud.

PAYNE, Frank Lynn. Lenaea, 1968. Ms., Univ. of Okla.
    In five brief sections, played without pause. Separat-
    ing the third and fourth sections is a "chance" section
    in which the players are given letter names and asked
    to improvise rhythms and melodic fragments.

PEARSON, William Dean (1905-   ). The Hunt. Chappell;
    Mc & M.

PEDERSEN, Paul. Wind Quintet. Can. Mus. Cent.

PEETERS, E. (1893-   ). Gothic Suite. Ms.? (GR).

PELEMANS, Willem (1901-   ). Quintet, 1948. Ms.? (R).

_____ . Second Quintet. Metropolis.

PELIKAN, Miroslav (1922-   ). Capricious Miniatures.
    (G).

PELZ. A Light Touch of Blue. Mc & M.

PEREZ IRIARTE, Narciso. Quintet, Op. 6, 1958. Lib.
    Cong.

PERINA, Hubert (1890-1964). Wind Quintet. (G).

PERISSAS, Madeleine (ca. 1910-   ). Scotch Suite. Andraud

PERLE, George (1915-   ). Quintet No. 1 Op. 37, 1959.
ACA.

_____ . Quintet No. 2 Op. 41, 1960. Presser.

PERSICHETTI, Vincent (1915-   ). Pastoral, Op. 21, 1943.
Schirmer, 1951; Mc & M.
A-4. A wonderful small piece in a delicate, advanced
tonal idiom.

PESSARD, Emile Louis (1843-1917). Prelude and Minuet.
Leduc.

_____ . Quintet (Aubade) Op. 6. Leduc, 1880.

PETERS, J. V. Seranata Fugata. Elder Conser.

PETERSON, Wayne. Metamorphosis for Wind Quintet. Ms.,
1085 View Way, Pacifica, Cal.

PETRIČ, Ivo. Quintet No. 1. Drustvo, 1964.

_____ . Quintet No. 2. Edicije Kompozitora.

PETROVICS, Emil. Fuvosötös. Ed. Musica, 1965; Zen.
Val.

PETRZELKS, Vilem (1889-   ). Divertimento, Op. 39
1942. Ms. ? (R).

PFEIFFER, G. (1835-1908). Pastorale, Op. 71. Andraud.

_____ . Three Petites Pieces. Andraud.

PHILLIPS, Peter (1930-   ). Music for Wind Quintet.
BMI.

_____ . Little Prelude and Blues, 1963. Lib. Cong;
MJQ Music.

PICHA, Frantisek (1893-1964). Wind Quintet, Op. 31, 1944.
(G), (V).

PIERCE, Edwin Hall (1868-   ). In Merry Mood. Gamble
Hinged; Mc & M.

_____ . Allegro Piacevole and Scherzo. Gamble Hinged;

Remick; Mc & M.

_____ . Short Quintet in B♭. Gamble Hinged; Mc & M.

_____ . Romance. Pro-Art, 1942.

PIERCE, V. Brent (1940-   ). Divertimento. Cont. Mus.
Proj.

PIERNE, Gabriel (1863-1937). (arr.   ). March of the
Little Tin Soldiers. Andraud.

_____ . Pastorale, Op. 14 No. 1. Leduc, 1887; South.
Mus. (And. Coll. - 22); Mc & M.
A short romantic piece featuring the oboe.

PIERNE, G. Paul. (1874-1952). Suite Pittoresque. Buffet-
Crampon; Mc & M.

PIETSCH, Edna Frida. Miniature Suite for Woodwind Quintet. Schmitt; Hall-McCreary.

PIJPER, Willem (1894-1947). Quintet, 1929. Donemus;
Mc & M.
AA-6. Four movements: Allegro, Adagio, Andante
moderato, Vivace.
Conflicting meter signatures and complex rhythms are
abundant; however, the piece is quite interesting.
Technically difficult.

PILSS, Karl (1902-   ). Serenade. Doblinger, 1957.

PISK, Paul (1893-   ). Quintet, Op. 96. ACA.

PISTON, Walter (1894-   ). Quintet, 1956. AMP, 1957;
Mc & M.
BB. Four movements: Animato, Contenerezzo, Scher-
zando, Allegro comodo.
A rather "dry" work in terms of melody and harmony.
Interest is generated by rhythmic elements and counter-
point.

PLACHETA, Hugo. Divertimento, Op. 8. Doblinger, 1965;
Mc & M.

PLEYEL, Ignace Joseph. (arr. Geiger). Rondo. Remick.

POLDINI, E.   93

_____. (arr. Harris). Quintet, Op. 48. Cundy-Bet-
toney.

POLDINI, E. (arr. Elkan). General Boom Boom. Elkan;
Mc & M.

POLDOWSKI, Lady Dean Paul. (arr. Barrere). Suite Miniature. Galaxy; Andraud.

POLÍVKA, Vladimír (1896-1948). Divertimento, 1939. (G).

PONC, Miroslav (1902-   ). Three Merry Pieces 1929.
(G).

PONSE, Luctor (1914-   ). Deux Pieces, 1943. Donemus;
Mc & M.

_____. Wind Quintet. Donemus.

POOT, Marcel (1901-   ). Symphonie, No. 2. Ms. (V).

_____. Concertino. Leduc, 1965; Mc & M.

PORSCH, Gilbert. Suite Modique. Remick; Mc & M.

PORTER, Cole. (arr. Harris). Quadrille. Mc & M.

PORTER, Quincy (1897-   ). Divertimento for Woodwind
Quintet. Peters, 1962; Mc & M.
BB-5. Four movements: Moderato serioso; Andante;
Scherzando; Adagio.
The score looks interesting, but the piece seems dull.

POSADA-AMADOR, Carlos (1918-   ). Quintet, 1958.
Ms., (CA).

POWELL, M. Divertimento. Mc & M.

PRAAG, Henri C. van (1894-   ). Quintet, 1938. Donemus.

_____. Quintet, No. 2, 1948. Donemus.

PRESSER, William. Minuet, Sarabande and Gavotte.
Presser; Mc & M.

PURCELL, Henry (1658-1695). (arr. R. Taylor).

Abdelazer.   South.   Mus.

_____ .   (arr.   ).   Trumpet Voluntary.   (HO),   New Art
Wind Quintet.

PURDIE,   Hunter.   Canon Apertus.   Pro Art,   1968.

PYLE,   Francis.   Quintet,   1960.   Ms. ,   (N),   Drake Univ.

QUICK,   George James.   Monostructure,   1967.   Lib.   Cong.

QUINET,   Marcel (1915-   ).   Eight Short Pieces.
CeBeDeM;   Mc & M.

_____ .   Quintet.   CeBeDeM;   Mc & M.

RACKLEY,   Lawrence.   Two Madrigals and a Jig.   Composers Autograph Publ.

RAIGORODSKY,   Natalia.   Introduction and Reflection for
Woodwind Quintet.   (N).

RAJTER,   L'udovit (1906-   ).   Wind Quintet,   1946.   (G).

_____ .   Wind Quintet,   1962.   (G).

RAMEAU,   Jean Phillipe.   (arr. Desormiere).   Acante et
Céphise.   Leduc.

_____ .   (arr. Nakagawa).   L'Agacante and L'Indiscrète.
Mc & M.

_____ .   (arr. Oubradous).   Symphonies and Dances.
Leduc;   Mc & M.

_____ .   (arr. Lockhart).   Tambourin.   Mus.   Pub.   Holding Corp;   Mc & M.

RAMSEY,   Gordon.   Mirror and Bagatélle,   1967.   Lib.   Cong.

RANDERSON,   Horace Edward (1892-   ).   Quintet.   Durand.

RANIER,   Priaulx (1903-   ).   Six Pieces.   Schott;   AMP;
Mc & M.

RANKI,   György.   Pentaerophonia,   Three Pieces.   Mc & M.

RANTA, Sulho (1901-   ).   Quintet.   Ms. ? (R).

RAPOPORT, Eda.   Indian Legend.   AMP, 1949; Mc & M.

RASHANIS, F.   Suite.   Russ. St. , 1961.

RATHAUS, Karol (1895-1954).   Gallant Serenade.   B & H,
1949; Mc & M.

RAVEL, Maurice.   (arr.   ).   Mother Goose Suite.   (HO),
New Art Wind Quintet.

_____.   (arr. Intravaia).   Pavane pour une Infante defunte.
Elkan-Vogel; Mc & M.

_____.   (arr. Kessler).   Piece en form de Habanera.
Leduc; Baron.

READ, Gardner (1913-   ).   Scherzino, Op. 24, 1935.
South. Mus. 1953.

_____.   Quintet.   Ms. , School of Mus. , Boston Univ.

REDDING, James.   Quintet.   (K), Ms. , Mich. State Univ.

REICHA, Anton (1770-1836).   Adagio.   Ms. , Paris Cons.

_____.   Trios Andante.   Ms. , Paris Cons.

_____.   Concertante.   Ms. , Paris Cons.

_____.   Quintet, Op. 88, No. 1.   Schott; Costallat.

_____.   Quintet, Op. 88, No. 2.   Mc & M.

_____.   Quintet, Op. 88, No. 3.   Schott; Costallat.

_____.   Quintet, Op. 88, No. 4.   Schott; Costallat.

_____.   Quintet, Op. 88, No. 5.   Mc & M.

_____.   Quintet, Op. 88, No. 6.   Schott; Costallat.

_____.   Quintet, Op. 91, No. 1.   Kneusslin, 1960; Costal-
lat; Mc & M.
    AA-6. No. 1 (No. VII) in C Major.   Four movements:
    Allegretto; Andante; Minuetto; Allegro.

An excellent quintet. The tempo markings are Reicha's own, making the fast movements amazingly fast. Instrumentalists of Reicha's time must be regarded with great respect.

_____. Quintet, Op. 91, No. 2. Costallat.

_____. Quintet, Op. 91, No. 3. Costallat; Mc & M.
AA-6. A brilliant classic-romantic major work. Difficult. Four movements.

_____. Quintet, Op. 91, No. 4. Costallat; Mc & M.

_____. Quintet, Op. 91, No. 5. Costallat; Mc & M.

_____. Quintet, Op. 91, No. 6. Costallat.

_____. Quintet, Op. 99, No. 1. Costallat.

_____. Quintet, Op. 99, No. 2. Costallat; Musica Rara, 1968, ed. Vester.
AA-6. 1. Larghetto-Allegro; 2. Andante; 3. Minuetto; 4. Allegro poco vivace--edited by F. Vester.
A difficult, but wonderful quintet. This opus is full of small, interesting sections, unusual in Reicha's works.

_____. Quintet, Op. 99, No. 3. Costallat.

_____. Quintet, Op. 99, No. 4. Costallat.

_____. Quintet, Op. 99, No. 5. Costallat.

_____. Quintet, Op. 99, No. 6. Costallat.

_____. Quintet, Op. 100, No. 1. Chex l'auteur (and some reprints).

_____. Quintet, Op. 100, No. 2. Chex (see above).

_____. Quintet, Op. 100, No. 3. Chex (see above).

_____. Quintet, Op. 100, No. 4. Chex; Mc & M.

_____. Quintet, Op. 100, No. 5. Chex.

_____. Quintet, Op. 100, No. 6. Chex.

REICHEL, A. Two Quintets. Andraud.

REICHEL, Bernard (1901-   ). Prelude, Passacaille et
    Postlude, 1951. Ms. , (V).

REIF, Paul (1910-   ). Kaleidoscope (with optional narra-
    tor). Seesaw Press 1966.

_____. Wind Spectrum. Seesaw Press 1966.

REINHOLD, O. Blaserquintett. Mc & M.

REITER, Albert. Musik fur Fünf Bläser. Doblinger, 1963;
    Mc & M.

REIZENSTEIN, Franz (1911-   ). Quintet. B & H, 1937;
    Mc & M.

RENZI, A. Five Bagatelles. Musica Rara.

RESSEGER, Robert. Quintet No. 1. Ms. , Sibley Lib.

REULING, Wilhelm (1802-1879). Quintets. Schott (R).

REUTTER, Georg (1708-1772). Windquintet. (V).

REVUELTAS, S. (1899-1940). Suite. South. Mus.

_____. Two Little Pieces. South. Mus. ; Chester.

REY, Cemal Reshid (1904-   ). In 5/8 Time, 1934. Ms. ?
    (R).

REYNOLDS, Roger. Gathering. Peters, 1964.

REYNOLDS, Verne. Quintet, 1964. Mills, 1967.
    AA-6. Four movements: Lento; Adagio; Vivace; Al-
    legro sciolto. Time: 20 mins. A major work for
    quintet. It is a strong work, excellently written, but
    not avant garde. Difficult.

RHODES, Phillip. Suite for Five Winds. ACA.

RIDKY, Jaroslav (1897-1956). Quintet, Op. 41, 1945.
    Ms. ? (R).

RIEGGER, Wallingford (1885-1961). Bläserquintett, Op. 51.

Ars Viva Verlag, 1952. Mc & M.

_____ . Three Canons for Woodwinds. Durand.

RIETI, Vittorio (1898-   ). Quintet, 1957. AMP; Mc & M.
BB-5. Four movements: Allegro moderato; Allegretto; Sostenuto; Allegro con brio.
An uncomplicated musical piece enjoyable to hear. It
is possibly good for theatre. Medium difficulty.

_____ . Woodcuts for Five Woodwinds. Gen. Mus. , 1968.

RIETZ, J. (1812-1877). Quintet. Ms. ? (GR).

RIISAGER, Knudåge (1897-   ). Quintet, 1921. (V).

_____ . Quintet, 1927. Ms. , (V).

RIMSKY-KORSAKOFF, Nicolas. (arr. Trinkaus). Flight of
the Bumblebee. Franklin.

RINCK, J. Quintet. Cor; Mc & M.

RISTIĆ, Milan (1908-   ). Quintet. (V).

RODGERS & HAMMERSTEIN. (arr. Harris). March of the
Siamese Children. Mc & M.

ROETSCHER, Konrad. Quintet, Op. 41. B & B, 1964
Mc & M.
ROHE, Robert. Quintet, 1957. Lib. Cong.

ROHOZINSKY, Ladislav (1886-1938). Quintette Pastorale.
Ms. , (V).

ROIKJER, Kjell (1901-   ). Kvintet, Op. 42. Skand.
Musfor. 1957.

ROMBERG, Andreas Jakob (1767-1821). Eight Quintets.
Ruhle & W.

RÖNTGEN, J. (1855-1932). Serenade. Ms. ? (GR).

ROOS, Robert de (1907-   ). Incontri voor Blaasquintet.
Donemus, 1966.

ROPARTZ, J. Guy (1864-1955). Two Pieces. Durand,

1926; Mc & M.

RORICH, Carl (1859-1941). Quintet, Op. 58.   Zimmerman,
1921.
ROSENBERG, Hilding. Quintet, 1959.   Stim.

ROSENTHAL, Lawrence. Quintet.   Chappell.

_____. Commedia.   Chappell, 1964.

ROSETTI, Francesco Antonio (1746-1792) (see also Rossler).
Quintet in E^b.   Presser, 1962; Kneusslin, 1961; Mc & M.
B-5. 1. Allegro; 2. Andante; 3. Allegro (rondo).
A good, but not great work.   The work is actually not
a transcription.   The French Horn part was originally
for tenor oboe.

ROSHER, Arnold. Woodwind Quintet.   Ms., (W).

ROSSEAU, Norbert (1907-   ).   Quintet, Op. 54.   CeBeDeM;
Mc & M.

RÖSSLER, Franz Anton (1746-1792).   Wind Quintet in E^b.
Kneusslin, 1961.
Same comment as for Rosetti above.

_____. (ed. Philadelphia Woodwind Quintet).   Rosetti
Quintet.   Presser, 1962.

ROTA, Nino (1911-   ).   Petite Offrande Musicale.   Leduc,
1955; Mc & M.

ROUSSAKIS, Nicolas. Woodwind Quintet No. 1.   ACA.

RUBENSTEIN, Anton G. Quintet, Op. 5.   Sansone.

RÜDLINGER, Gottfried. Divertimento, Op. 45.   (V).

RUGOLO, P. Bossa-Waltz.   Alcove, 1965; Mc & M.

RUSCH, Milton. Quintet, 1964.   Ms., Univ. of Wis. -
Milwaukee.
BB-6. A large scale twelve-tone piece using most of
the 20th Century compositional devices.   Not outstanding, but of interest to the performers.   The five movements are played without pause.

RUSSELL, Armand.   Quintet.   Ms., Mich. State Univ.

RUYNEMAN, Daniel.   Nightingale Quintet, 1949.   Donemus.

_____.   Reflexions, No. 4, 1961.   Donemus.

RYCHLÍK, Jan. (1916-1964).   Suite, 1945.   (G).

_____.   Wind Quintet, 1960.   Artia.

SABALYEV, B. W.   Suite.   Russ. St., 1966.

SACHSE, Hans Wolfgang (1899-   ).   Quintet, 1954.   (V).

SACHSZE, Hans (1891-1960).   Bläser-Suite, Op. 32.   Böhm, 1935.

SAEGUSA, Shigeaki.   Blaserquintett.   Lib. Cong.; Pub. in Tokyo, 1964.

SAGAEV, Dimitur.   Quintet No. 1, 1964.   Lib. Cong.

SAIKKOLA, Lauri (1907-   ).   Divertimento.   Ms.? (R).

SALGADO, Luis H. (1903-   ).   Quintet, 1958.   Ms., (CA).

SALICH, Milan (1927-   ).   Wind Quintet, 1962.   (G).

SALMENHAARA, Erkki (1941-   ).   Quintet.   Finnish Mus. Council.

SALZEDO, L. (1921-   ).   Divertimento, Op. 40.   Lopes Ed.

SANTA CRUZ, Dominga (1899-   ).   Quintet.   Peer; 1967.

SANTO, Samuel Benjamin (1776-   ).   Twenty-four Pieces.   Ms.? (R).

SANTOLIQUIDO, F. (1883-   ).   Pezzi Due (Nocturne and Pastorale).   Cor., 1963; Mc & M.

SANTORO, Claudio (1919-   ).   Quintet, 1942.   Ms., (CA).

ŠATRA, Antonin (1901-   ).   Three Aquarelles, 1960.   (G).

SAUER, Eugene Edwin (1931-   ).   Suite of Little Pieces,

1956. Lib. Cong.

SAUTER, E. Dedicatto a Shinolo, 1956. Priv. , N. Y. , (V).

SCARLATTI, Allesandro (1660-1725). (arr. R. Herder).
A Scarlatti Sonata (Longo 465). AMP.

SCARLATTI, Domenico (1685-1757). (arr.). Suite in F.
Mc & M.

SCARMOLIN, A. Louis. Badinage. Belwin, 1941; Mc & M.

_____. By the Sleepy Nile. Gamble Hinged, 1941; Mc
& M.

_____. Scherzino All'Antica. Pro Art.

_____. Rustic Dance. Barnhouse.

SCHABBEL, Will (1904-   ). Bagatellen. (V).

SCHAEFER, Theodor (1904-   ). Quintet, Op. 5. Pazdirek, 1940.

SCHAFER, George. Quintet. Ms. , (McA).

SCHAT, Peter (1935-   ). Quintet, 1960. Donemus.

_____. Improvisations and Symphonies. Donemus.

SCHELB, Joseph (1894-   ). Quintet. Ms. , (V).

SCHERRER, H. (1865-   ). (arr. Andraud?). Old French
Dances, Op. 11. South Mus. (And. Coll. - 22).

_____. Altfranzösiche Tänze, Op. 11. Schmidt, 1899.

SCHIBLER, Armin (1920-   ). Kaleidoskop, Op. 41.
Simrock, 1956.

SCHIERBECK, Paul (1888-1949). Capriccio, Op. 53. Hansen, 1951.

SCHIFFMAN, Harold. Allegro con spirito di San Niccolo.
AMP.

_____. Divertimento for Woodwind Quintet. PP, Jan. 1970.

102 The Woodwind QuintetThe Woodwind Quintet

SCHINDLER, Gerhard (1921-   ). Divertimento Notturno.
Modern Ed. , 1957.

SCHISKE, Karl (1916-   ). Blaserquintett, Op. 24. Doblinger, 1959; Universal Ed. ; Mc & M.

SCHLEMM, Gustav Adolf. Blaserquintett. Grosch, 1963

SCHMID, Heinrich Kasper (1874-1953). Blasquintett, Op. 28.
Schott, 1921; Mc & M.
    AA-5. 1. Allegro; 2. Grazioso amabile; 3. Moder-
    ato-Allegro giusto.
    These three movements of good romantic "Viennese"
    style music are excellently composed. They fit the
    quintet well and are enjoyable to hear.

SCHMIDEK, Kurt. Sonatine, Op. 31. Doblinger.

SCHMIT, Camille (1908-   ). Quintet. Ms. ? (R).

SCHMITT, Florent (1870-1958). Chants alizes, Op. 125.
Durand, 1955; Mc & M.

SCHMITT, Nicholas (ca. 1802-   ). Three Quintets. Pleyel.

SCHMUTZ, Albert D. Scherzo poetique. Cundy-Bettoney;
Mc & M.

SCHNEEWEIS, Jan. (1904-   ). A Children's Suite, 1955. (G).

SCHNEIDER, Horst. Quintet, 1958. (V).

SCHÖNBERG, Arnold (1874-1951). Quintett, Op. 26. Universal Ed. , 1925; Mc & M.

SCHOUWMAN, Hans (1902-   ). Nederlandse Suite, Op.
40b, 1943. Donemus.

SCHREMM, Harold. Quintet. Ms. ? (W).

SCHRÖDER, Hanning (1896-   ). Divertimento, 1957.
Peters.

SCHUBERT, Franz (1797-1828). (arr. Holmes). Allegretto.
Barnhouse.

_____ . (arr.   ). Ballet Music, Rosamunde. Andraud.

_____ . (arr. Springer). Hark, Hark, the Lark. Mus.
Pub. Hold.

_____ . (arr. L. Taylor). March Hongroise. Mills.

_____ . (arr.   ). Minuet. Andraud.

_____ . (arr.   ). Scherzo, Op. 166 (and Buononcini
Rondeau). Andraud; Mc & M.

_____ . (arr. Schoenbach). Shepherd Melody. Mc & M.

_____ . (arr. Elkan). Valse Sentimentale. Elkan; Mc
& M.

_____ . (arr. R. Taylor). Who is Sylvia (and) An die
Nachtingall. South. Mus.

SCHUBERT, Heino. Musik fur five Bläser. Mann. Musik.

SCHULLER, Gunther (1925-   ). Quintet, 1958. AMP,
1965.

_____ . Suite. Jos. Marx, 1957; Mc & M.
A-4. Three movements: Prelude, Blues, Tocatta.
Written when Schuller was young. The writing is clear
with few problems. The second movement, Blues
(2:10) is an outstanding encore.

SCHULTZ, Svend (1913-   ). Une Amourette, petite Serenade. Skand. Musfor, 1954; Mc & M.

SCHUMANN, Richard. Pastoral, 1936. Lib. Cong.

SCHUMANN, Robert (1810-1856). (arr. Sarlit). Fughette
and Gigue. Baron.

_____ . (arr.   ). Knight Rupert (and Gossec-Tam-
bourine). Andraud; Mc & M.

_____ . (arr.   ) New Year's Song. Andraud; Mc & M.

SCHUTZ, Albert D. Scherzo Poetique. Cundy-Bettoney.

SCHWAKE, Kurt Karl von. Quintet, 1925. Ms. , (V).

SCHWARTZ, Elliott. Interruptions. Ms. , Bowdoin Coll.
Uses tape in last movement.

SCHWARZ, Leonid. Oriental Suite, 1932. Russ. Musikver.
Un. Ed.

SCHWERTSICK, Kurt. Eichendorf Quintet. Un. Ed.
With piccolo.

_____. Proviant. (V).

SEARCH, Frederick P. Chinese Dance. ACA.

SEEGER, Ruth Crawford. Suite for Wind Quintet. Univ. of
N. Car., Lark Woodwind Quintet, Summer 1969.

SEHLBACH, Erick (1898-   ). Kortum-Serenade, Op. 30.
Moseler, 1952.

SEIBER, Matyas. Permutazione a Cinque, 1958. Schott;
Mc & M.

_____. Quintet. Musica Rara.

SEIDL, Jan. (1908-   ). Two Quintets. Ms.? (R).

SEMMLER, Alex. Quintet. Ms. ? (HO).

SENAILLE, Jean Baptiste. (arr. L. Taylor). Rondo Serioso. Mills.

SEREBRIER, Jose. Little Suite. Chester.

_____. Pequena Musica. South. Mus.; 1961 Mc & M.

ŠESTÁK, Zdeněk (1925-   ). Cassation in D#, 1958. (G).

_____. Concertino, 1964. (G).

SETER, Mordecai (1916-   ). Diptyque. Isr. Mus. Inst.

SHAFTER, George. Woodwind Quintet. (K), Ms. Mich.
State Univ.

SHAPEY, Ralph (1921-   ). Quintet, 1964. Ms., (W).

_____. Movements. ACA.

SHARMAN, Grant. Quintet. New Music.

SHEPHERD, Arthur (1880-1958). <u>Divertissement, 1943.</u>
Ms., Cleveland Institute of Mus.

SHERMAN, Robert W. (1921-   ). <u>Quintet, 1963.</u> Ms.,
(N), Ball State.

SHOSTAKOVICH, Dmitri (1906-   ). (arr.   ). <u>Polka.</u>
(HO) New Art Wind Quintet.

SHULMAN, Alan. <u>Folk Songs.</u> Ms.? (HO).

SIBELIUS, Jean (1865-1957). (arr. R. Taylor). <u>Berceuse.</u>
South. Mus.

_____. (arr. Langenus). <u>Pastorale from "Pelleas."</u>
Andraud; Mc & M.

SICCARDI, Honorio (1897-   ). <u>Tres Cantos Argentinos,</u>
<u>1953.</u> Ms., (CA).

SIEGMEISTER, Elie (1909-   ). <u>Quintet, 1932.</u> Ms.

SIENNICKI, Edmund. <u>Allegro.</u> B & H, 1966.

SILLIMAN, A. Cutler. <u>Quintet No. 2.</u> Ms., State Univ.
N.Y. - Fredonia.

SIMON, Joseph. <u>Quintet.</u> Ms.? (HO).

SKERJANC, Lucijan (1900-   ). <u>Quintet.</u> Ms.? (R).

SKILTON, Charles S. <u>Sarabande.</u> Ms.? (HO).

SKORZENY, Fritz. <u>Eine Nachtmusik, 1963.</u> Doblinger,
1965; Mc & M.

SLATES, Philip. <u>Sonatina.</u> Ms., (McA).

SMATEK, Miloš (1895-   ). <u>Wind Quintet.</u> (G).

_____. <u>Scherzino.</u> (G).

SMETÁČEK, Václav (1906-   ). <u>Wind Quintet, 1930.</u> (G).

_____. <u>Mood Pictures, 1932.</u> (G).

_____. <u>The Davle Polka.</u> (G).

_____ . Perpetuo Brilliante.   (G).

_____ . Aus dem Leben der Insekten.   Continental Ed.
    1939.

SMITH, Donald. Quintet. Shawnee.

SMITH, Leland C. (1925-   ). Quintet, 1947. Ms., (R).

SMITH, Russell. Woodwind Suite, 1956. ACA.

SNYDER, Randell. Quintet. Ms., Univ. of Wis.
    Two movements: Slowly; Scherzo.
    The piece is pointalistic atonal (possibly twelve-tone).
    It looks interesting on paper, but aurally result is
    uninteresting. Difficult.

SOBECK, Johann (1831-1914). Quintet, Op. 9. B & B,
    1879.

_____ . Quintet, Op. 11. Bosworth, 1891.
    BB-5. Four movements: Andante; Andante sostenuto;
    Allegretto; Larghetto.
    Typical classic-romantic writing. Rather uninteresting
    for concert purposes. Of medium difficulty with no
    unusual ensemble problems. Very good for training
    purposes.

_____ . Quintet, Op. 14. Bosworth, 1891.

_____ . Quintet, Op. 23. Lehne, 1897; Ehrler.

_____ . Quintets 11 and 14 (movements published sepa-
    rately). Belwin.

_____ . "Lucia di Lammermoor" Quintet. Andraud.

SÖBER, Ants. Quintet, 1968. Lib. Cong.

SODDERLAND, Jan (1903-   ). Quintet. Donemus.

SODERO, Cesare (1886-1947). Morning Prayer. AMP, 1933;
    Mc & M.

_____ . Valse Scherzo. AMP, 1933; Mc & M.

SOMARY, Johannes. Quintet, 1957. Ms., (W).

SOMERS, Harry (1925-   ). Quintet, 1948. BMI.

_____ . Movement, 1957. Ms., (CA).

SOMIS, Giovanni Battiste. (arr. Hernried). Adagio and
    Allegro. Fischer; Mc & M.

SORRENTINO, Charles. Beneath the Covered Bridge. Mills,
    1963.

SOUKUP, Vladimïr (1930-   ). Wind Quintet, 1957. (G).

SOURIS, Andre (1899-   ). Rengaines, 1937. Leduc, 1955;
    Mc & M.

SOWERBY, Leo (1895-   ). Pop Goes the Weasel 1927.
    Fitzsimmons, 1930; Mc & M.

_____ . Quintet, 1916. Schirmer, 1931.

_____ . Quintet, 1930. Lib. Cong.

SPENCER, O. W. Playtime. G. F. Briegel.

SPETH, H. Capriccio, 1950. (V).

SPIES, Leo (1899-   ). Sonata, 1959. (V).

SPISAK, Michal (1914-   ). Quintet, 1948. Ms. ? (R).

SPRONGL, N. Woodwind Quintet, Op. 90. Doblinger, 1965;
    Mc & M.

SRAMEK, Vladimir (1923-   ). Five Quintets, (1951-1961).
    Ms., (V).

STAEMPFLI, Edward (1908-   ). Quintet. Ms. ? (R).

_____ . Variations, 1950. Ms. ? (R).

STAINER, Charles (ca. 1900-   ). Scherzo, Op. 27.
    Rudall & Carte, 1929; Mc & M.

_____ . Improvisation. Schott.

STARER, Robert. Serenade. Ms. ? (HO).

STARK, Robert (1847-1922).   Quintet, Op. 44.   Oertel.

STEARNS, Peter Pindar.   Quintet for Winds.   ACA.

STEEL, Christopher.   Divertimento.   Novello.

STEGGALL, R.   (1867-1938).   Quintet, Op. 21.   Ms. ?   (GR).

STEIN, Leon (1910-   ).   Quintet, 1937.   ACA.

STEVENS, Noel.   Quintet, Op. 10.   Ms.

STEWART, Kensey D.   (1933-   ).   Two Movements for
    Woodwind Quintet.   Cont. Mus. Proj.

STEWART, Robert.   Two Movements.   ACA.

_____.   Five Visions.   ACA.

_____.   Three Pieces.   ACA.

Stockhausen, Karlheinz.   No. 5 Zeitmase.   Presser; Un. Ed.
    1957.

STONE, David (1922-   ).   Prelude and Scherzetto.   No-
    vello, 1956.

STORP, Sigmund Hans (1914-   ).   Kammermusik, 1960.
    Moseler, 1962.

STRADELLA, Alessandro (1642-1682).   (arr. ?)   Sonata in G.
    Camara; Mc & M.

STRAESSER, Ewald.   Quintet.   Ms. , (HO).

STRAIGHT, Willard.   Quintet, 1959.   Ms. , (W).

STRENS, Jules (1892-   ).   Quintet.   Ms. ?   (R).

STRINGFIELD, Lamar (1897-   ).   An Old Bridge, 1936.
    Leeds.

_____.   A Moonshiner Laughs.   Andraud; Mc & M.

_____.   Virginia Dare Dance.   Ms. ?   (R).

STRONG, Templeton (1856-1948).   Aquarelles.   Ed. du

Siecles Musical.

STRUBE, Gustav (1867-1953). Quintet, 1930. Lib. Cong.

STRUNZ, Jacob (1783-1852). Quintets. Ms. ? (R).

STÜP'.ER, Bruno (1892-1958). Quintet. Ms. ? (R).

⌐ ᴊCHON, Eugen (1908-   ). Serenade, Op. 5, 1932. Ms. ? (R).

SUCHY, Frantisek (1902-   ). Quintet, 1928. (G).

_____. Three Czech Dances 1952. (G).

_____. Concertante Quintet 1947. (G).

_____. Quintet, 1958. (G).

_____. Wind Quintet, 1936. B & H.

SUTER, Hermann (1870-1926). Quintet. (V).

SUTER, Robert (1919-   ). Quatre Etudes, 1962. Ed. Henn-Chapuis, 1962.

SVOBODA, Jiři (1897-   ). Wind Quintet, 1942. (G).

SWACK, Irwin. Quintet. Ms. ? (R).

SWANSON, Howard. Night Music. Ms. ? (HO).

SWEELINCK, Jan Pieters. (arr. Ernest Lubin). Variations on a Folksong. B & H; Mc & M.

SYDEMAN, William (1928-   ). Quintet No. 1. Seesaw Press 1967.

_____. Quintet No. 2. Mc & M.

_____. Texture Studies for Quintet. Seesaw Press.

SZALOWSKI, Antoni (1907-   ). Quintet. Omega Music, 1956; Mc & M.
SZEKELY, Endre (1912-   ). Quintet. Mills.

_____. Quintet No. 2. Editio Musica, 1965.

SZELIGOWSKI, Tadeusz (1896-   ). Kwintet. Polskie Wyd.
Muz. 1955.

SZERVANSKY, Endre (1912-   ). Fuvosötös, 1953. Zen.
Val. 1957; B & H; Mc & M.

_____ . Quintet No. 2. Zen Val. ; B & H 1960.

TAFFANEL, Paul (1884-1908). Quintet. South. Mus. (And.
Coll. - 22) Mc & M.
   AA-6. A first rate romantic composition for wood-
   wind quintet.

TAKACS, Jenö (1902-   ). Eine Kleine Taffelmusik,
Op. 74? or 27. Mc & M; Doblinger.
   AA-5. Five movements: Molto Vivace; Andante;
   Presto; Andante; Presto. Time 14:30.
   An excellent program piece with contrasting and inter-
   esting movements. Modern sounding without being
   avante. Medium to difficult.

TAKATA, Saburo (1913-   ). Suite, 1952. Ms. ? (R).

TAL, Joseph. Quintet. (V).

TANENBAUM, Elias (1924-   ). Sonatina. ACA.

_____ . Quintet No. 2. ACA.

TAPPER, T. Three Minuets. Kalmus.

TARANOV, Gleb. Quintet, Op. 38. L. C. Mockba, 1965.

TARTINI, Giuseppe (1692-1770). (arr. Trinkaus). Arioso
in e. Kay & Kay; Franklin; Andraud.

_____ . (arr. Trinkaus). Evening Song. Kay & Kay;
Franklin; Andraud.

_____ . (arr. Trinkaus). Largo from Violin Sonata in g
minor. Mus. Pub. Hold. ; Mc & M.

TAYLOR, Lawrence. Suite Miniature. Gamble Hinged,
1940; Mc & M.

TELEMANN, George Philip (1681-1767). (arr. Hinnenthal).
Overture Suite. Leuckart; Andraud; Mc & M.

TEMPLETON, Alex. (arr. Wm. Rhoads). Passepied.
   A small light musette-like piece, which seems decep-
   tively easy considering the endurance problem for several instruments.

TEPPER, Albert (1921-   ). Dance Souvenirs. Seesaw
   Press.

_____ . Minuet No. 1, 1948. Lib. Cong.

_____ . Minuet No. 2, 1948. Lib. Cong.

THIERAC, Jaques (1896-   ). Sonatina, 1960. (V).

THILMAN, Johannes (1906-   ). Asporismen. Br & H,
   1966.

_____ . Bläserquintet, Op. 44a. Mitteld. Verl. 1951;
   Mc & M.

THOMAS, Charles. (arr. Trinkaus). Gavotte from Mignon.
   Franklin.

TICHY, O. A. (1899-   ). Quintet. Ms. ? (GR).

TIESSEN, Heinz (1887-   ). Divertimento, Op. 51. Kistner.

_____ . Kleine Schularbeit, Op. 43a. Ms? (R).

TOEBOSCH, Louis (1916-   ). Sarabande e Allegro, Op.
   71. Donemus, 1959.

TOLDI, Julius. Little Suite. Ms., (HO).

TOMAN, Josef (1894-   ). Two Wind Quintets. (G).

TOMASI, Henri (1901-   ). Cinq (5) Dances. Leduc,
   1963; Mc & M.

_____ . Quintette. Lemoine, 1952; Mc & M.

_____ . Variations on Corsican Theme. Leduc, 1938;
   Mc & M.

TOMKINS. (arr.   ). Two English Keyboard Pieces.
   Mills.

TORJUSSEN, Trygve. Norwegian Wedding Dance. Schmidt.

TOSAR, Hector A. (1923-   ). Divertimento, 1957. Ms.,
(CA).

TREDE, Yngve Jan. Le Chant des Oiseaux. Ugrino Verlag,
1959.

_____ . Quintet. Ugrino Verlag, 1959.

TREMBLAY, George (1911-   ). Two Quintets, 1940.
ACA.

TREXLER, Georg (1903-   ). Spitzweg Suite, 1956. Br.
& H.

TROJAN, Vaclav (1907-   ). Dechovy Kvintet, Op. 8,
1937. Statni 1956.

_____ . Quintet on Czech National Airs. Ms.? (WM).

TSCHAIKOWSKY, Peter I. (1840-1893). (arr. R. Taylor).
Suite in "Album for Winds." South. Mus.
    AA 4-5. Time: 15 mins.
    Nocturne; Feuillt d'Album; Chant sans Paroles; Am
    Kamin; Humoresque; Chant sans Paroles; Danse Russe.
    Delightfully melodic music, well-arranged and not too
    difficult. Excellent for concert and training. Nothing
    similar in the quintet literature.

_____ . (arr.   ). Melody, Op. 42, No. 3. Mc & M.

_____ . (arr. Nakagawa). Three Dances: Mazurka, Op.
39 - 10, Polka Op. 39 - 14, Waltz Op. 39- 8. AMP.

_____ . (arr. R. Taylor). Suite No. 1. Mc & M.

_____ . (arr. Trinkaus). Andante Cantabile. Mc & M.

TULL, Fisher. Suite for Woodwind Quintet. Shawnee Press.

TURECHEK, Edward. Introduction and Scherzo. Witmark,
1933; Mc & M.

TURNER, Godfrey. Suite. Ms.? (HO).

TUTHILL, Burnet C. (1888-   ). Sailor's Hornpipe Op. 14,

No. 1, 1935. C. Fischer, 1937; Mc & M.

_____ . Variations, Op. 9. Sansone.

TYLŇÁK, Ivan (1910-   ). Wind Quintet, 1947. (G).

_____ . Wind Quintet, 1958. (G).

ULLRICH, Josef (1911-   ). Ball Slippers. (G).

ULRICH, Hugo. Masterworks for Woodwinds. Eble (HO).

URAY, Ernst L. (1906-   ). Schladminger Tänze. Doblinger.
_____ . Music fur Bläserquintet. Doblinger, 1966.

URBANEK, Rudolf (1907-   ). A Grotesque Polka. (G).

URBANNER, E. Etude fur Bläser. Doblinger, 1966.

VALEN, Fartein (1887-1952). Serenade, Op. 42. Hinrichson; Mc & M.

VALENTE, William E. (1934-   ). Divertimenti. Cont. Mus. Proj.

VAN DE MOORTEL, L. Preludio and Canzone. Mc & M.

VAN DER VELDEN, Renier (1910-   ). (see Velden, van der). Divertimento, 1939. Ms. ? (R) (First Concerto 1939?) Maurer?

_____ , Second Concerto. Mc & M.

VAN HULSE, C. (1897-   ). Quintet, Op. 3. Shawnee.

VAN PRAAG, Henri C. (1880-   ). Quintet, 1938. Donemus; Mc & M.

_____ . Quintet, 1948. Donemus, 1949; Mc & M.

VAN VACTOR, David (1906-   ). Divertimento, 1936. Ms., (CA).

_____ . Gavotte, 1940. Ms., (CA).
A-4. Allegretto - 69-72.
A small movement in classical form with Prokofiev-like harmonic and key relationship. Delightful as a

part of a group or as an encore.

_____ . Suite for Woodwind Quintet. PP, Jan. 1970.

_____ . Quintet, 1959. Ms. , (CA).

VAN VLIJMEN, Jan. Quintetto, 1958. Donemus, 1960.

VAUBOURGOIN, Jean Fernand (1880-1952). Quintet. (V).

VAZZANA, A. E. Quintet. Ms. , Univ. of Wis.

VEERHOFF, C. H. Quintet No. 1. AMP.

_____ . Quintet No. 2. AMP.

VEGA, Aurelio De La (1925-   ). Quintet, 1957. Ms. ,
(CA).

VELDEN, (van der) Renier (1910-   ). First Concerto,
1939. Maurer.

_____ . Second Concerto. Metropolis, 1957; Mc & M.

VERNEUIL, Raoul de (1899-   ). Quintet. Ms. ? (R).

VERRALL, John (1908-   ). Serenade, 1944. Music
Press, 1947; Mc & M.

_____ . Serenade, No. 2, 1954. ACA.

VILLA-LOBOS, Heitor (1887-1959). Quinteto, 1928. Eschig;
Mc & M.
A continuous piece with varying tempos. A major concert piece in the advanced tonal idiom of Villa-Lobos'
late technic.

VINCZE, Imre (1926-   ). Divertimento. Ed. Musica,
1965.

VINTNER, Gilbert (1909-   ). Sonata for Wind Quintet.
Polyphonic Reproductions.

_____ . Two Miniatures. B & H, 1950; Mc & M.

VLIJMEN, Jan van. Quintetto, 1958. Donemus, 1960.

VOGEL, Wladimir (1896-   ). Quintet, 1941. Ms. ? (R).

VON KREISLER, Alexander. Two Portraits. Southern 1967.

_____ . Triptych. Southern 1967.

_____ . Chorale, Prelude and Fugue. Southern, 1966.

_____ . Pastorale. Southern, 1965.

_____ . Fable. Southern, 1965.

_____ . Possum Trot. Southern, 1965.

_____ . Humorous March. Southern, 1965.

_____ . Quintet. South. Mus. , 1964; Mc & M.

VOSS, Frederich (1930-   ). Capriccioso. Br. & H, 1966.
     (flute solo)

VOXMAN, H. and HERVIG, ed. Ensemble Repertoire (col-
     lection). Rubank; Mc & M.

VREDENBURG, Max (1904-   ). Au pays des Vendanges
     1951. Donemus, 1955.

_____ . Suite Breve. Musica Rara.

VUATAZ, Roger. Musique pour 5 Instruments á vent, Op.
     48. Odeon, 1953.

WAGNER, Richard (1813-1883). (arr. R. Taylor). Album-
     blatt. South. Mus.

_____ . (arr.   ). March from Tannhauser. (HO), New
     Art Wind Quintet.

WAHLICH, Marcel. Quintet. (V).

WALKER, Richard (1912-   ). Adagio and Allegro.
     Barnhouse, 1953.

_____ . In Joyous Mood. Barnhouse, 1954.

WALTERS, H. Waggery for Woodwinds. (HO).

WALZEL, L. M. Quintet, Op. 42. Doblinger.

WARD, William R. Little Dance Suite. Mills, 1949.

WARD-STEINMAN, David. Montage for Woodwind Quintet.
ACA.

WASHBURN, Robert. Quintet for Winds. Oxford U. Press.

_____ . Quintet No. 2, 1963. Ms. , (N).

_____ . Suite. Presser; Mc & M.

WATERSON, James. Quintet. Lafleur, 1922.

WEBER, Alain (1930-   ). Quintette. Leduc, 1956; Mc &
M.

WEBER, C. M. v. (arr. Kesner). Rondo. Remick; Mus.
Pub. Hold. Gamble Hinged; Mc & M.

WEBER, Joseph Miroslav (1854-1906). Quintet, 1900. Ms. ?
(R).

WEBER, Ludwig (1891-1947). Quintet. Ms. ? (R).

WEIGEL, Eugene (1910-   ). Short, Slow and Fast, 1949.
Ms. ? (R).

WEIGL, Vally. Mood Sketches. ACA.

WEIS, Flemming. (1898-   ). Serenade. Hansen, 1941.

WEISS, Adolph (1891-   ). Vade Mecum, 1959. Ms. , (C).

_____ . Quintet, 1931. ACA.

WELLESZ, Egon (1885-   ). Suite, Op. 73. Lengnick,
1950; Mc & M.

WESTON, P. Arbeau Suite. Concord. Mus. ; Elkan, 1969;
Mc & M.

WHARTON, John. Quintet. Ms. , (HO).

WHEAR, Paul. Quintet, 1956. Leblanc, 1964.

WHETTAM, Graham. Quintet, Op. 19. de Wolfe.

WHITE, Donald. Three for Five. Shawnee.

WHITTENBERG. Games of Five. Ms. , Univ. of Conn.

WHITTENBERG, Charles. Quintet. Ms. , (V).

WIJDEVELD, Wolfgang (1910-   ). Quintet, 1934. Donemus.

WILDER, Alex (1907-   ). Quintet No. 1. Ms. , Wilder
Mus.

_____. Quintet No. 2. Ms. , Wilder Mus.

_____. Quintet No. 3. Schirmer; Mc & M.

_____. Quintet No. 4. Ms. , Wilder Mus.

_____. Quintet No. 5. Ms. , Wilder Mus.

_____. Quintet No. 6. Ms. , Wilder Mus.

_____. Quintet No. 7. Ms. , Wilder Mus.

_____. Quintet No. 8. Ms. , Wilder Mus.

_____. Quintet No. 9. Ms. , Wilder Mus.
AA-5. Four movements: 1. $\downarrow$ = 104; (3 mins.)
2. $\downarrow$ = 192 (2 mins. 5 sec.); 3. Swinging $\downarrow$ = 120
(3:25); 4. Slow (3:20.
An excellent quintet. Not too difficult. Dedicated to
Wingra Quintet.

_____. Suite for Quintet. Ms. , Wilder Mus.

_____. Suite for non-voting Quintet. Ms. , Wilder Mus.

WILDSCHUT, Clara (1906-1950). Kleine Serenade. Donemus.

WILEY, Charles. Quintet, 1950. Ms. , (N).

WILLIAMS, Clifton. Concert Suite. South. Mus. , 1966.

WILLIAMS, David Russell.   Fanfare.   Ms., Sibley Lib.

WILSON, Donald M.   Stabile II.   ACA.
(For combination of two or more high and one or more
low instruments.)

WINSTEAD, William.   Woodwind Quintet.   Ms., Univ. of
West Virginia.

WIRTH, Helmut.   Kleine Clementiade Scherzo.   Mc & M.

_____ .   Heiteres Spiel, 1937.   Hüllenhagen, 1953.

WISSE, Jan (1921-   ).   Limitazioni II, 1962.   Donemus.

WISSMER, Pierre.   Quintette.   Ricordi, 1965.

WITHERSPOON, Valerie (1943-   ).   Woodwind Quintet.
Ms., Univ. of Wis.

WOLSTENHOLME, William (1865-1931).   Quintet.   Ms.?
(R).

WOLTER, Detlef.   Thema mit Variationen.   C. F. Kahnt,
1963.

WOOD, Charles (1866-1926).   Quintet.   B & H, 1933.

WOOD, Thomas (1892-1950).   The Brewhouse at Bures.
Stainer & Bell, 1929.

WOOLLEN, Russell (1923-   ).   Quintet, 1955.   Mc & M.

WOOLLETT, Henry.   Quintet.   Ms., (HO).

WUILLEUMIER.   Quintet.   Andraud.

WUORINEN, Charles (1938-   ).   Movement.   Presser,
1963; Mc & M.

_____ .   Wind Quintet.   ACA.

YODER, Paul.   Relax.   Mc & M.

_____ .   (arr.   ).   Dry Bones.   Mc & M.

YORK, Walter Wynn.   Neo-Gothics.   Pyraminx.

ZAFRED, Mario   119

ZAFRED, Mario (1922-   ). Quintet. Ricordi.

ZAGWIJN, Henri (1878-1954). Quintetto, 1948. Donemus;
   Mc & M.

ZAMECNIK, John. Allegro Guibiloso. Sam Fox, 1937.

ZANINELLI, L. Dance Variations. Shawnee, 1962; Mc &
   M.

_____ . Musica Drammatica. Shawnee, 1968.

ZELENKA, Istvan. Chronologie. Doblinger, 1966.

ZELINKA, Jan Evangelista (1893-   ). Air Free of Charge,
   1933. (G).

ZENDER, Hans (1936-   ). Quintett, Op. 3. B & B, 1953;
   Mc & M.

ZICH, Jaroslav (1912-   ). Quintet. Ms. ? (R).

ZILCHER, Herman (1881-1948). Quintet, Op. 91. Muller,
   1894; Mc & M.

ZILLIG, Winfried (1905-   ). Lustspielsuite, 1934. Bar.

ZIPP, Frederich (1914-   ). Serenade. Möseler.

ZOELLER, Carl (1840-1889). Quintet, Op. 132. W. D.
   Cubitt Son, 1883.

ZRNO, Felix (1890-   ). Three Wind Quintets. (G).

_____ . Suite, 1962. (G).

WOODWIND QUINTET

PLUS ONE INSTRUMENT

Woodwind Quintet and Piano

ALARY, Georges (1850-1929). Sextet. Durdilly.

ANDRIESSEN, Jurriaan (1925-   ). L'Incontro di Cesare e
Cleopatra, 1956. Donemus.

ARRIEU, Claude (1903-   ). Concerto. Ricordi.

BADINGS, Henk (1907-   ). Sextet, 1952. Donemus.

BENJAMIN, Arthur L. Jamaican Rumba. B & H.

BIZET, Georges (1838-1875). (arr. Wilson). Quintet from
Carmen. C. Fischer.

BLUMER, Theodor (1882-   ). Sextet, Op. 45 F. Simrock, 1922.

          . Sextet (Kammersymphonie), Op. 92. Wilke,
1943; Ries & Erler.

BOISDEFFRE, Rene De. Sextet, Op. 49 (cb ad lib). Hamelle,
1894.

BRAUER, Max (1855-1918). Sextet - g. Br. & H, 1920;
AMP.

BRESCIA, Domenico. Suite. Lib. Cong.

BRETON Y HERNANDEZ, Tomas (1850-1923). Sextet,
(c. 1900) Union Mus. Espagnola.

BRIGHT, Houston. Woodwind Quintet and Piano. Shawnee.

BRUNEAU, Earnest. Sextet C. Schneider, 1904.

BULLERIAN, Hans (1885-   ). Sextet, Op. 38 - G^b.
Simrock, 1925.

CASADESUS, Robert (1899-   ). Sextet. Durand.

COHN, James. Sextet. Ms., Lib. Cong.

COLOMER, B. M. Caprice Moldave.

CORDS, Gustav. Sextet. Andraud.

CRUFT, Adrian. Dance Movement (Ballabile). Elkan, 1964.

DAVID, Johann Nepomuk (1895-   ). Divertimento, Op. 24. Br. & H, 1940.

DESPORTES, Yvonne (1907-   ). Prelude and Pastorale. Andraud.

DONOVAN, Richard. (1891-   ). Sextet, 1932. Ms.

DRESDEN, Sem (1881-1957). Kleine Suite - C, 1913. deWolfe.

_____. Suite d'Aprés Rameau, 1916. deWolfe.

_____. Third Suite, 1920. deWolfe.

DUKELSKY, Vladimir (1903-   ). Nocturne. Fischer.

FARRENC, Louise (1804-1875). Sextet, Op. 40.

FLAMENT, Edouard (1880-1958). Poème Nocturne, Op. 7. Evette.

FRANCAIX, Jean (1912-   ). Sextet. Schott.

FRENSEL-WEGENER, Emmy (1901-   ). Sextet, 1927. Donemus.

FRID, Geza (1904-   ). Sextet. Donemus.

FUHRMEISTER, Fritz. Gavotte und Tarantelle, Op. 6. Zimmerman.

GENIN, T. Jeune. Sextet - E^b. Demets, 1906; Eschig.

GODRON, Hugo (1900-   ). Serenade, 1947. Donemus.

GÖRNER, Hans Georg (1908–   ). Kammermusik, Op. 29.
Peters; Litolff.

GREENBERG, Lionel. Sextet. Can. Mus. Cent.

HARRIS, Roy (1898–   ). Fantasy, 1932. Arrow.

HEMEL, Oscar van (1892–   ). Sextet, 1962. Donemus.

HILL, Edward Burlingame (1872-1960). Sextet, Op. 39,
1934. Schirmer, 1939; Galaxy.

HOLBROOKE, Josef (1878–   ). Sextet, Op. 33a. Riorden, 1906; Chester 1906, 1922.

HUBER, Hans (1852-1921) Sextet - B^b, 1900. Hug, 1924.

HUFFER, Fred K. Sailor's Hornpipe. Witmark.

HUSA, Karol. Serenade (for piano or harp). Leduc; Elkan·
Vogel.

INDY, Vincent d' (1851-1931). (arr.   ). Sarabande et
Minuet, Op. 24bis (Op. 72), 1918. Hamelle.

JACOB, Gordon (1895–   ). Sextet. Musica Rara, 1962.

JACOBI, Wolfgang (1894–   ). Suite, Op. 21. Ms.

JENTSCH, Walter (1900–   ). Kleine Kammermusik, Op.
5 (Thema mit Variationen). Ries & Erler, 1935.

JONGEN, Joseph (1873-1953). Rhapsody, Op. 70, 1922.
CeBeDeM; Chester.

JUON, Paul (1872-1940). Divertimento, Op. 51, F, 1913.
Lienau, 1913; Schlesinger.

KAHOWEZ, Günther. Structures pour 6 Instruments.

KEITH, George D. Journey of the Swagmen. Mc & M.

KLENGEL, Auguste A. Polonaise Concertante, Op. 35.
Fetis.

KOHN, Karl. Serenade, 1962. Private.

126

KOPPEL, Herman David (1908-   ). Sextet, Op. 36.
Skand. Musfor, 1947.

KOX, Hans (1930-   ). Sextet, No. 3, 1959. Donemus.

_____ . Sextet, No. 4. Donemus.

KREUTZER, Konrad. (1780-1849). Sextet. by Composer,
Paris.

LACROIX. Sextet. Ms., Curtis Institute.

LADMIRAULT, Paul (1877-1944). Variations sur un Choral,
1935. Lemoine, 1952.

LAKNER, Yehoshua (1924-   ). Sextet, 1951. Isr. Mus.
Inst., 1962.

LEGLEY, Victor (1915-   ). Sextet, Op. 19, 1945.
CeBeDeM, 1954; Brogneaux, Maurer, 1956.

MAJOR, J. Gyula (1858-1925). Sextet, Op. 39. Ms.

MARGOLA, Fr. Sonatina a Sei. Mc & M.

MARTINU, Bohuslav (1890-1959). Sextet. Statni.

MARVEL, Robert. Sextet. Ms., State Univ. of N.Y.-
Fredonia.

MENDELSSOHN-BARTHOLDY, Felix. Scherzo, Op. 118.
Andraud.

_____ . (arr. Jospe). Intermezzo from Midsummer
Night's Dream. C. Fischer.

_____ . (arr. Jospe). Scherzo, Op. 110. C. Fischer.

MEULEMANS, Arthur (1884-   ). Aubade, 1934. CeBe-
DeM; Maurer, 1957.

MIGNONE, Francisco (1897-   ). Sextet, 1935. Escola
National de Musica, 1937.

MILLER, Ralph Dale. Three American Dances, Op. 25.
Fischer, 1949.

MOULAERT, Raymond (1875-1962).   Concert, 1950.
CeBeDeM.

_____ .   Sextet, 1925.   CeBeDeM.

MOZART, W. A. (1756-1791).   K. 608 (instrum. Pijper).
Donemus.

MULDER, Ernest W. (1898-1959).   Sextet, 1946. Donemus.

OSIECK, Hans (1910-   ).   Divertimento, 1950. Donemus.

PIJPER, Willem (1894-1947).   Sextet, 1923. Donemus.

POULENC, Francis (1899-1963).   Sextet, 1932/39. Hansen,
1945.

POUWELS, Jan (1898-   ).   Sextet, 1958. Donemus.

QUEF, Charles.   Suite, Op. 4.   Noël, 1902.

REED, Owen H.   Symphonic Dance.   Mills, 1963.

REUCHSEL, Amedée (1875-1931).   Sextet. Lemoine, 1909.

RHEINBERGER, Josef (1839-1901).   Sextet, Op. 191^b, F.
Leuckart, 1900.

RIEGGER, Wallingford (1885-1961).   Concerto, Op. 53, 1953.
AMP, 1956.

RIISAGER, Knudåge (1897-   ).   Concertino, Op. 28^a.
Norsk.

ROLDAN, A. (1900-1939).   Sextet. Chester.

ROOS, Robert de (1907-   ).   Sextet, 1935. Donemus.

ROUSSEL, Albert (1869-1937).   Divertissement, Op. 6, 1905.
Rouart, 1906, 1948; Salabert.

SCHADEWITZ, Karl (1887-1945).   Sextet, 1924. Ms.

SCHRÖDER, Herman (1904-   ).   Sextet, Op. 36, 1957.
Schott, 1959.

SEITZ, Albert.   Two Sextets.   Andraud; Carl Geist.

SHANKS, Ellsworth. Nightmusic for Six. MPHC; Gamble⁻
Hinged.

SMIT, Leo (1900-1945). Sextet, 1933. Donemus.

SOWERBY, Leo. Pop Goes the Weasel. Fitzsimmons.

STRATEGIER, Herman (1912-   ). Sextet, 1951.
Donemus.

STRIEGLER, Kurt (1886-1958). Sextet, Op. 58, (E^b).
Ms., L. B., Dresden.

SUGÁR, Reszö (1919-   ). Frammenti Musicali. Ed.
Musica, 1963.

TANSMAN, Alexandre (1900-   ). Danse de la Sorcière.
Eschig; Schott.

THUILLE, Ludwig. Sextet, Op. 6 (B^b). Br. & H, 1889,
1955.

TREXLER, Georg (1903-   ). Sextet, 1958.

TUTHILL, Burnet Corwin. Variations "When Johnny Comes
Marching Home," Op. 9, 1934. Galaxy, 1934.

ULTAN, Lloyd. Two Movements for Piano Sextet. PP,
Jan. 1970.

VELDEN, Renier van der (1910-   ). Sextet, 1948.
Metropolis.

VELLONES, Pierre (1889-1939). A Versailles, Op. 60, No.
7. Baron; Regia, 1934.

VIOLETTA, Wesley la (1894-   ). Sextet, 1940.

WAGNER, Richard. (arr. Boyd). An Album Leaf. C.
Fischer.

WEISS, Adolph (1891-   ). Sextet, 1947. ACA.

WHETTAM, Graham. Fantasy Sextet. Wolfe.

WILLNER, Arthur. Sextet. Andraud.

WINNUBST, J. (1885-1934).   Kleine Serenade, 1924.
  Donemus.

ZAGWIJN, Henri (1878-1954).   Suite, 1912.   Donemus.

_____.   Scherzo, 1946.   Donemus.

Woodwind Quintet and Woodwind Instrument

FLUTE (and Picc.)

HUGBRECHTS, Albert (1899-1938). Sextet (Pastorale), 1927.
    CeBeDeM.

ENGLISH HORN

MALHERBE, Edmond (1870-   ). Sextet, Op. 31. Ms. ,
    Curtis Institute.

MAPES, Gordon. Passacaglia. Ms. , Curtis Institute.

CLARINET

BEETHOVEN, Ludwig. (arr. Schoenfeld). Scherzo, Op. 10,
    No. 2. MHPC.

_____ . (arr. Schoenfeld). Finale, Op. 10, No. 2.
    MHPC.

_____ . (arr. Schoenfeld). Scherzo, Op. 27, No. 2.
    MHPC.

_____ . (arr. Schoenfeld). Scherzo, Op. 2, No. 3.
    MHPC.

BILLINGS, B. Chester. C. Fischer.

CARMICHAEL, Hoagi. (arr. Klickmann). Stardust. Mills.

DAVIES, Peter Maxwell (1934-   ). Alma Redemptoris
    Mater, 1957. Schott.

DEVASINI, G. Sextet. Ricordi, 1843.

FROSCHAUER, H. Sextet. Doblinger.

GAN, N. K. Kinderbilder Suite. Russ. St. , 1955.

JENSEN, Niels Peter. (arr. Klickmann). Bridal Song.
Standard.

JETTEL, Rudolf (1903-   ). Sextet. Rubato, 1949.

KLEINSINGER, George (1914-   ). Design for Woodwinds.
BMI, 1946; AMP.

LABATE, Bruno. Intermezzo and Scherzino in A. Labate.

LEFEBVRE, Charles Edouard (1843-1917). Second Suite,
Op. 122. Leduc; Andraud.

MENTER,   Serenade. Andraud.

MOUQUET, Jules. Suite. Lemoine.

TARTINI, Giuseppe. (arr.). Largo from Sonata in g.
Witmark.

BASS CLARINET

JANACEK, Leos. Mladi (Youth) Suite, 1924. Hud. Mat. ,
1925; Artia, 1958.

KARREN, L. Three Humoristic Scenes. Andraud.

REBNER, Wolfgang E. Sextett. Modern Ed. , 1962.

THOMPSON, Virgil. Barcarolle, 1940. Mercury, 1948.

BASSOON

JAVAULT, Louis (early 19th cent.). Six Sextets. Gaveaux.

SOP. SAXOPHONE

ANGELINI, Louis (1935-   ). Woodwind Sextet. Cont.
Mus. Proj.

ALTO SAXOPHONE

DUBOIS, Pierre Max. Sinfonia de Camera. Leduc, 1965.

GRABNER, Hermann. Sextet, 1932. Kistner & Siegel.

HEIDEN, Bernard. Sextet. NACWPI, 1970.

STEIN, Leon. Sextet. Camara.

TOMASI. Printemps. Leduc.

Woodwind Quintet and One Brass Instrument

TRUMPET

ACHRON, Joseph (1886-1943). Sextet, Op. 73, 1938. New Music, 1942.

ARTSIBOUSHEV, Nicolai. (arr. Klingman). Mazurka in F. Standard.

BEREAU, J. S. Sextet. Choudens.

BOSSI, Renzo (1883-1965). Tema Variato, Op. 10. Böhm, 1939.

READ, Gardner. Nine by Six, 1951. Ms., School of Mus., Boston Univ.

SCHUMANN, Robert (arr. Cafarella). Little Hunting Song, Op. 68, No. 7. MHPC.

SCHWERTSICK, Kurt. Proviant.

SUTERMEISTER, Heinrich (1910-). Serenade No. 2, 1961. Schott.

HORN

ALLERS, Hans-Günther. Suite. Möseler.

ALTMAN, Eddo. Kleine Tanz Suite. Hofmeister.

BEETHOVEN, Ludwig von. (arr. Cafarelli). Scherzo, Op. 2, No. 2. MPHC.

REINECKE, Karl (1824-1910). Sextet, Op. 271. Zimmerman, 1904; Sansone.

STUTSCHEWSKY, Joachim (1891-). Sextet, 1959. Priv., Tel. Aviv.

TUBA

WILDER, Alex.   Effie joins a Carnival.   Camara, 1966.

Woodwind Quintet and String Instrument

VIOLIN SOLO

ETLER, Alvin. Concerto. AMP.

VIOLIN

KANITZ, Ernest. Sextet, 1932. Ms. , (HO), Univ. S. Cal.

SUCHÝ, František. (1902-   ). Concertino, 1931. (G).

ZRNO, Felix (1890-   ). Suite, "Wandering of Folk Musicians" 1956. (G).

VIOLA

POLIVKA, Vladimir (1896-1948). Suite, 1933. Ms.

VACEK, Karel Václav (1908-   ). Bagatelle. (G).

CONTRA BASS

HARTLEY, Walter. Sextet. Priv. , 16 Boundary Ave. , Elkins, W. Va.

LADERMAN, Ezra (1924-   ). Sextet in One Movement. ACA.

MÜLLER, Ludwig Richard. Tanzerische Impressionen. Br. & H.

POLOLANIK, Zdeněk (1935-   ). Musica Spingenta, 1961.

VRÁNA, František (1914-   ). Fables, 1962. (G).

HARP (or Piano)

HUSA, Karol. Serenade. Elkan-Vogel.

HARP

ADDISON, John. Serenade. Oxford Univ. Press, 1958.

MONKENDAN. Suite in C. Donemus.

VAN BUSKIRK, Carl. Esoteric Suite, 1950. Univ. of Indiana (HO).

WEN-CHUNG, Chou. Suite for Harp and Wind Quintet. PP, Jan. 1970.

Woodwind Quintet and Voice

SOPRANO

ADLER, Samuel (1928-   ). Songs with Winds. Oxford
    Univ. Press (rental only).

SCHAFER, R. Murray. Minnelieder. Ms.
    AA-5. A group of songs in old Dutch. The idiom is
    enjoyably modern.   Outstanding music.

TENOR

JONES, Wendal. Songs for Wind Quintet and Tenor. Ms.,
    E. Wash. College.

NARRATOR

REIF, Paul. Kaleidoscope (with optional narrator). See-
    saw Press.

HIGH VOICE

SUCHÝ, František. Moravian and Slovak Folk Songs, 1954.
    (G).

Woodwind Quintet and One Instrument

CHORUS

RACKLEY, Lawrence. Prologue and Ceremonial Dance.
PP, Jan. 1970.

PERCUSSION

JIRÁSEK, Ivo (1920-   ). Wind Quintet. (G).

SCULTHORPE. Tabuhtabuhan for Wind Quintet and Percussion. Adelaide Quintet.

TAPE

BOTTJE, Will G. (1925-   ). Three Etudes for Woodwind
Quintet and Tape, 1963. Available from composer; South.
Ill. Univ. at Carbondale. 17 minutes.

4 SOUND TRACKS

LEEUW, Ton de. Antiphonie, 1960. Donemus.

WOODWIND QUINTET
AND TWO INSTRUMENTS

Woodwind Quintet and Two Instruments

PIANO, CLARINET

BEETHOVEN, Ludwig von (arr.). Scherzo, Op. 10, No. 2. Witmark.

BILLINGS, B. Chester. C. Fischer.

PIANO, BASS CLARINET

GOLD, Ernest. Septet. Benjamin.

PIANO, CONTRA BASSOON

ONSLOW, George (1784-1853). Septet, Op. 79 (B^b). Kistner, 1852.

PIANO, TRUMPET

MIROUZE, Marcel. Piece en Septour. Leduc, 1953.

SAUGUET, Henri (1901-   ). Dix Images pour une vie de Jeanne d'Arc, 1943. Ms.

PIANO, VIOLIN

KŘIĆKA, Jaroslav (1882-   ). Concertino, Op. 76, 1940. Ms.

PIANO, CELLO

BLANC, Adolphe. Septet, Op. 54. Costallat; Richault.

PIANO, CONTRA BASS

BOISDEFFRE, Charles Henri René de (1838-1906). Sextet,
  Op. 49. Hamelle, 1894.

KITTL, Johann Friedrich (1806-1868). Septet, Op. 25 (E^b).
  Kistner, 1846.

PIJPER, Willem (1894-1947). Septet, 1920. Donemus.

PIANO, NARRATOR

BOTTJE, Will Gay (1925-   ). Diversions, 1961; 6 Thurber
  "Further Fables of our Time." ACA.

PIANO, PERCUSSION

BERRY, Wallace. Divertimento for Wind Quintet, Piano and
  Percussion. Elkan-Vogel.

DOST, Rudolf (1877-   ). Septet, Op. 55 (G). Zimmerman,
  1923.

PIANO, TAMBUR

PIERNE, Gabriel (arr.) March of the Little Tin Soldiers.
  Leduc; Andraud.

PIANO, TYMPANI

DOST, Rudolf (1877-   ). Septet, Op. 56. Baxter-Northrup.

PERSICHETTI, Vincent. Septet, Op. 35, 1948. Ms.

FLUTE, CLARINET

DUBOIS, Theodore (1837-1924). Au Jardin: Petite Suite.
  Heugel, 1908.

FLUTE, BASSOON

PIERNÉ, Gabriel (1863-1937). Preludio et Fughetta, Op.40.
  Durand; Elkan Vogel.

DRIESSLER, Johannes. 143

ENGLISH HORN, BASS CLARINET

DRIESSLER, Johannes. Aphorismen, Op. 7ª. Bar.

ENGLISH HORN, BASSOON

FLAMENT, Edouard (1880-1958). Fantaisie et Fugue, Op.
28. Evette; Andraud.

ENGLISH HORN, ALTO SAX

KOECHLIN, Charles (1867-1951). Septet, Op. 165, 1937.
L'Oiseau Lyre.

CLARINET, BASSOON

INDY, Vincent d' (1851-1931). Chanson et Danses Op. 50,
1898. Durand.

MAYR, S. In the Morning. Andraud.

MOQUET, Jules (1867-1946). Suite. Lemoine, 1910;
Andraud; Baron.

RHENE-BATON, (1879-1940). Aubade, Op. 53. Durand, 1940.

CLARINET, ALTO SAX

DUBOIS, Theodore (1837-1924). Sinfonia da Camera.
Elkan-Vogel.

CLARINET, HORN

BUSCH, Carl. An Ozark Reverie. Fitzsimmons.

MORTELMANS, Lodewijk (1868-1952). Le Berger Solitaire.
Het Musiek.

TOJA, Giovanni (c. 1800). Serenata. Ricordi.

WATSON, W. C. Divertimento. Witmark.

WIND, Blasius. Serenade Amusante, Op. 1339. Andraud.

CLARINET, TROMBONE

FROMMEL, Gerhard (1906-   ). Suite, Op. 18. Müller.

BASS CLARINET, TRUMPET

HINDEMITH, Paul (1895-1963). Septet, 1948. Schott, 1949.

SPRONGL, Norbert (1892-   ). Septet. Priv., Vienna.

BASSOON, HORN

HABERT, Johannes E. (1833-1896). Scherzo, Op. 107.
   Br. & H; AMP.

RÖNTGEN, Julius (1855-1932). Serenade, Op. 14 (A).
   Br. & H, 1878.

BASSOON, TRUMPET

PIERNE, Gabriel (1863-1937). Pastorale Variée, Op. 30.
   Durand.

BASSOON, CELLO

WIDERKEHR, Jacques C. M. Symphony Concertante, Op. 4.
   Cotelle; Fetis.

HORN, TRUMPET

BRUGK, Hans-Melchior (1909-   ). Divertimento, Op. 29.
   Simrock.

HORN, HARP

BUMCKE, Gustav. Love and Sorrow, Op. 24. Andraud;
   Diem., Saturn-Verlag.

ROOTHAM, Cyril Bradley (1875-1938).   Septet, 1930.   Ms.

TRUMPET, TROMBONE

BORRIS, Siegfried (1906-   ).   Intrada Serena, No. 1.
   Sirius.

COSCIA, Silvio (possibly Coscia Silvio).   Septet.   Mc & M.

DOUÈ, Jean (1922-   ).   Septet, 1953.   Heugel.

PABLO, Luis de (1930-   ).   Coral, Op. 2.   Modern.

SYLVIUS, Coscia.   Septet.   Baron, 1953.

TRUMPET, CONTRA BASS

NEUKOMM, Sigismund Ritter von (1778-1858).   Septet,
   c. 1832.   Mc & M.

VIOLIN, CELLO

YUN, Isang (1917-   ).   Music for Seven Instruments, 1959.
   B & B.

VIOLIN, CONTRA BASS

BAAREN, Kees van.   Septet, 1952.   Donemus.

VIOLA, HARP

ROOTHAM, Cyril Bradley (1875-1938).   Septet.   Andraud.

HARP, CELESTE

ZAGWIJN, Henri.   Nocturne, 1918.   Donemus.

WOODWIND QUINTET
AND THREE INSTRUMENTS

PIANO, TRUMPET, TROMBONE

THILMAN, Johannes Paul (1906-   ). News for Winds and Piano. Priv. 1962.

PIANO, ENGLISH HORN (bass Clarinet), TRUMPET

SCHWAEN, Kurt (1909-   ). Concertino Apollineo. Litolff; Peters.

PIANO, HORN, XYLOPHONE

HAYASAKA, Fumio. Suite in Seven Parts with Eight Instruments. Pub. in Tokyo.

FLUTE, CLARINET, BASSOON

DALLEY, Orien E. Reverie. Witmark, 1933.

DUBOIS, Theodore (1837-1924). 1 ère Suite. Heugel, 1898.

_____ . 2 ème Suite. Leduc, 1898.

FLUTE, CLARINET, HORN

ZOPF. Serenade, Op. 35, No. 2. Ms., (HO).

FLUTE, BASSOON, HORN

EBERWEIN, Traugott M. (1775-1831). Musique d'Harmonie. Ms. LB-Darmstadt.

PETYREK, Felix (1892-1951). Divertimento, 1923. Andraud.

WEINGARTNER, Felix.   Octet, Op. 73.   Chester;   Birnbach.

FLUTE, BASSOON, TRUMPET

PASCAL, Claude.   Octet.   Durand, 1947.

PIERNE, Gabriel.   Pastorale Variee.   Durand.

OBOE, CLARINET, BASSOON

KLING, Henri.   Spring Poetry, Idyl.   Andraud.

SCARLATTI, Alessandro.   (arr.)   Allegro from Eighth Suite.
Ricordi.

STIEBER, Hans (1886-   ).   Spielmusik, No. 3.   Hofmeister, 1953.

ENGLISH HORN, BASSOON, HORN

LAZZARI, Sylvio (1857-1944).   Octet, Op. 20.   Evette, 1920;
Buffet.

ENGLISH HORN, BASS CLARINET, TRUMPET

BRUSSELMANS, Michel (1886-1960).   Prelude et Fugue 1923.
Salabert.

CLARINET, BASS CLARINET, HORN

CAMPBELL-WATSON, Frank.   Divertimento.   Witmark;
MHPC.

INGALLS, Albert M.   Woodwind Octet.   Ms., (HO) 6551
24th Ave. NE, Seattle, Wash.

CLARINET, BASSOON, HORN

DOMANSKY, Alfred (1883-   ).   Octet.   Ms.

GOUVY, Louis Theodore (1819-1898). Octet, Op. 71 (E♭).
Kistner, 1882.

HARTMANN, E. Serenade, Op. 43. Ries & Erler.

HAYDN, Franz Joseph (1732-1809). Adagio. Cons. Cherubini.

HENNEBERG, Richard (1853-1925). Serenade. Ms. (pf.
red. Stockholm, 1918).

HOROWITZ, Joseph (1927-   ). Phantasy on a Theme of
Couperin, 1959. Mills.

LACHNER, Franz (1803-1890). Octet, Op. 156 (B♭). Kistner, 1850, 1873.

NOVÁCEK, Rudolf (1866-1900). Sinfonietta, Op. 48. Br. &
H, 1905.

REINECKE, Karl (1824-1910). Octet, Op. 216. Kistner,
1892.

SAINT-SAENS, Charles C. (arr. Taffanel). Album Leaves.
Durand; Elkan-Vogel.

SCHERER, Heinrich. Old French Dance, Op. 2. Baxter-
Northrup.

CLARINET, CONTRA BASSOON, HORN

FROMMEL, Gerhard (1906-   ). Suite, Op. 18. Müller.

CLARINET, BASSOON, TRUMPET

WAILLY, Paul de (1856-1933). Octet, Op. 22. Rouart,
1905; Baudoux; Salabert.

CLARINET, HORN, TRUMPET

GAL, Hans (1890-   ). Divertimento, Op. 22, 1924.
Leuckart, 1925.

CLARINET, TRUMPET, TROMBONE

ALLEN, Herbert Phillip (1883-1952). The Muses. Blake.

CLARINET, BASS CLARINET, TRUMPET

BEHREND, Fritz (1889-   ). Suite, Op. 116. Priv. , 1956.

BASS CLARINET, HORN, TRUMPET

BORRIS, Siegfried (1906-   ). Octet, Op. 25, No. 3.
Sirius.

HORN, TRUMPET, TROMBONE

PENTLAND, Barbara (1912-   ). Octet for Winds, 1948.
Can. Mus. Cent.

HORN, CORNET (trumpet), TROMBONE

CODIVILLA, F. Ottetto (E^b). Pizzi, 1919.

2 TRUMPETS, TROMBONE

ANGERER, Paul (1927-   ). Octet. Un. Ed.

FELLEGARA, Vittorio (1927-   ). Octet, 1953. Zerboni,
1955.

SCHAT, Peter (1935-   ). Octet, 1957. Donemus.

TRUMPET, TROMBONE, CONTRA BASS

VARÈSE, Edgar (1885-1965). Octandre, 1923. Curwin,
1924; Ricordi, 1956.

TRUMPET, CELLO, CONTRA BASS

NEUKOMM, Sigismund Ritter von (1778-1858). Octet.
Ms. , Boston Public Lib.

KUPFERMAN, Meyer   153

BASS CLARINET, VIOLIN, CONTRA BASS

KUPFERMAN, Meyer (1926-   ).   Chamber Symphonie.
   Mc & M.

VIOLIN, VIOLA, CELLO

SCHAEFER, Theodor.   Divertimento Mesto, Op. 22, 1946.
   Ms.

WAGENAAR, Bernard (1894-   ).   Concertino, 1942.
   Fischer.

WOODWIND QUINTET
AND FOUR INSTRUMENTS

Woodwind Quintet and Four Instruments

PIANO (4 hands), XYLOPHONE, SISTRO

RICCI-SIGNORINI, Antonio (1867-   ). Fantasia Burlesca.
Carisch, 1925.

PIANO, HORN, 2 TROMBONES

RYCHLIK, Jan (1916-   ). African Cycle, 1962. Statni,
1963.

PIANO, ENGLISH HORN,
BASS CLARINET, TRUMPET

CATURLA, A. G. (1906-1940) Primavera Suite Cubana,
1931. New Music, 1933.

2 FLUTES, CLARINET, HARP

LUIGINI, A. C. L. J. Andante Cantabile, Op. 41. Grus.

_____ . Aubade, Op. 13. Andraud.

FLUTE, OBOE, CLARINET, BASSOON

BIRD, William. Pavane. Ricordi.

KOSCHOWITZ, Josef (1800-   ). Six Hongroises. Ms.

PISTON, Walter (1894-   ). Divertimento, 1946. BMI,
1946.

FLUTE, OBOE, CLARINET, HORN

BERNARD, Emile. Divertissement. Sansone.

FLUTE, CLARINET, OBOE, HARP

BURGMEIN-MUGNONE.   "O Mama Cara" and Preghiera.
B & H.

FLUTE, CLARINET, BASSOON, HORN

SAINT-SAENS, C. Camille.   Deuxieme Suite.   Baxter-
Northrup.

OBOE, CLARINET, BASSOON, HORN

BEETHOVEN, Ludwig.   (arr. Hess).   Adagio and Allegro
fur die Spieluhr.   Br. & H.

BONVIN, Ludwig (1850-1939).   Melodie, Op. 56a.   Br. & H.

_____ .   Romance, Op. 19a.   Br. & H.

BRÄUTIGAM, Helmut (1914-1942).   Kleine Jagdmusik, Op.
11, 1938.   Br. & H, 1939, 1956.

FAURE, Gabriel Urbain.   (arr. Grovlez).   Nocturne Nonet,
Op. 33, No. 1.   Andraud.

GOOSSENS, Eugene.   Petite Symphony.   Costallat.

GOUNOD, Charles (1818-1893).   Petite Symphonie (B^b).
Costallat, 1904.

GOUVY, Louis Theodore (1819-1898).   Suite Gauloise, Op.
90.   Un. Ed., 1900.

GROVLEZ, Gabriel.   Nocturne.   Sansone.

LANGE, Fr. Gustav (c. 1861).   Nonet.   Seeling, 1879.

OTTEN, Ludwig (1924-   ).   Divertimento, No. 3, 1964.
Donemus.

PARRY, Charles Hubert (1848-1918).   Nonet, Op. 70, c.
1877.   Ms.

SCHOLZ, Robert.   Second Divertimento.   Ms., (HO), 55 W.
55th St., N.Y.C.

ENGLISH HORN, ALTO CLARINET, BARITONE SAX, HARP

BUMCKE, Gustav. Promenades, Op. 22. Ries & Erler;
Andraud.

CLARINET, BASSOON, HORN, TRUMPET

GOOSSENS, Eugene (1893-1962). Phantasy Nonet, Op. 36,
1924. Curwin, 1925; Leduc, 1962.

CLARINET, BASSOON, HORN, TROMBONE

FROHLICH, Theodor (1803-1836). Walzer. Ars Viva, 1954;
Muller.

HORN, TRUMPET, TROMBONE, TUBA

HOVHANNES, Alan (1911-   ). Tower Music, Op. 129.
Rongwen.

ACCORDION, TRUMPET, TROMBONE, TUBA

GERHARD, Roberto (1896-   ). Nonet. Keith Prowse,
1957; Mills.

FLUTE, CLARINET, HORN, CONTRA BASS

BRUN, G. (1878-   ). Passacaille, Op. 25. Lemoine,
1908; Andraud.

CLARINET, BASSOON, HORN, CONTRA BASS

NEUBAUER, Franz Christoph (1760-1795). Parthia (B^b),
1791. Ms. , (LB).

CLARINET, BASSOON, VIOLIN, CONTRA BASS

BRESGEN, Cesar (1913-   ). Jagdkonzert. Schott.

TRUMPET, VIOLIN, VIOLA, CELLO

MUSGRAVE, Thea (1928-   ). Chamberconcerto, 1962.
Chester.

2 VIOLINS, VIOLA, CELLO

ADASKIN, Murray (1906-   ). Rondino for Nine Instruments. Can. Mus. Cent.

HARSANYI, Tibor (1898-1954). Nonet, 1927. Sirene Mus.
1930; Eschig.

JONG, Marinus de (1891-   ). Nonet, Op. 33, 1929.
CeBeDeM.

MASSENET, Jules (1842-1912). Introduction et Variations.
Heugel.

RHODES. Ensemble Studies. Cont. Mus. Proj.

SAMAZEUILH, Gustav (1877-   ). Divertissement et Musette (g). Durand, 1912.

SCHOECK, Othmar (1886-1956). Serenade, Op. 1. Hug,
1907.

SCHRECK, Gustav (1849-1918). Nonet. Ms.

STRIEGLER, Kurt (1886-1958). Kammersymphonie, Op. 14.
Junne, 1912.

VIOLIN, VIOLA, CELLO, CONTRA BASS

BORCOVEC, Pavel (1894-   ). Nonet, 1941. Hud. Mat.,
1945.

BURGHAUSER, Jarmil (1921-   ). Nonet.

BURIAN, Emil Frantisek (1904-1959). Nonet, 1938.

DAVID, Thomas Christian (1925-   ). Concerto for Nine
Solo Instruments. Doblinger.

DOBIAS, Václav (1909-   ). Nonet "The Native Land."

Sadlo, 1953; Orbis.

FAGAN. Nonet.

FARRENC, Louise (1804-1875). Nonet, Op. 38. Ms.

FOERSTER, Josef Bohuslav (1859-1951). Nonet, Op. 147,
1931. Hud. Mat. , 1948; Bar.

FOLPRECHT, Zdenek (1900-). Concertino, Op. 21,
1940. Hud. Mat. , 1950; Bar.

GIURANNA, Barbara. Adagio e Allegro da Concerto.
Ricordi.

HABA, Alois (1893-). Nonet, Op. 40. Ms. , (V).

_____ . Nonet, Op. 41. Ms. , (V).

_____ . Nonet, Op. 82, 1953. Bar.

HABA, Karl (1898-). Nonet, Op. 32, 1948.

HLOBIL, Emil (1901-). Nonet, Op. 27, 1947. Hud.
Mat. ; Orbis, 1951.

JAROCH, Jiri. Detska Suita, Nonet, 1952 (Children's Suite).
Statni, 1956; Bar.

JIRAK, Karel Bohuslav. Variations, Scherzo and Finale,
Op. 45a, 1942. Ms. , (V).

KAREL, Rudolf. Nonet, 1945. Ms. , (V).

KREJČI, Iša (1904-). Nonet, 1937. Ms. , (V).

KRETSCHMER, Edmund. Nonet. Ms. , (V).

KVAPIL, Jaroslav (1892-1958). Nonet, 1944. Ms. , (V).

LACHNER, Franz (1803-1890). Nonet, 1875. Ms. , (V).

LEIBOWITZ, Rene (1913-). KammerKonzert, Op. 10,
1944. Un. Ed. , 1947.

MARTINU, Bohuslav (1890-1959). Nonet, 1958. Statni,
1959; Bar.

MOSER, Franz J. (1880-1939). Symphonie for Nine Solo Instruments, Op. 40. Doblinger, 1924.

NOVAK, Jan (1921-   ). Balletti à 9. Hud. Mat., 1959; Bar.

ONSLOW, George (1784-1853). Nonet, Op. 77. Kistner; Joubert, 1851.

OSTERC, Slavko (1895-1941). Nonet, 1937. Ms., (V).

PAUER, Jiri (1919-   ). Divertimento. (V).

PETRŽELKA, Vilém (1889-   ). Nonet, Op. 42. Ms., (V).

RHEINBERGER, Josef (1839-1901). Nonet, Op. 139. Kistner, 1885.

RIDKÝ, Jaroslav (1897-1956). Nonet, Op. 32, 1934. Sadlo, 1941.

_____. Nonet, Op. 39, 1943. Hud. Mat., Bar.

SPOHR, Ludwig (1784-1859). Nonet, Op. 31. Peters, 1858, 1954; Litolf, 1954; Bar, 1959.

SROM, Karol (1904-   ). Fairy Tales for Nonet, 1952. Artia, 1963.

_____. Etudes for Nonet. Statni, 1965.

ZICH, O. (1879-   ). Chod Suite. Hud. Mat.

VIOLIN, VIOLA, CELLO, HARP

BUTOW, Leo (1896-   ). Kammersymphonietta, Op. 1. Ms., (V).

WOODWIND QUINTET
AND FIVE INSTRUMENTS

Woodwind Quintet and Five Instruments

PIANO, TRUMPET, VIOLIN, VIOLA, CELLO

LUTYENS, Elizabeth (1906-   ). Six Tempi for Ten Instruments, Op. 42. Mills, 1959.

PIANO, 2 VIOLINS, VIOLA, CELLO

PRATELLA, Franco-Balilla (1880-   ). Par un dramma Orientale, Op. 40. Ricordi, 1938.

WOLF-FERRARI, Ermanno. Kammersymphonie, Op. 8. Rahter, Andraud.

PIANO, TRUMPET, TROMBONE, VIOLIN, VIOLA

PRAUSNITZ, Frederick. Episode. New Music, 1949.

FLUTE, OBOE, CLARINET, BASSOON, HORN

ANDRIESSEN, Jurriaan (1925-   ). Respiration Suite. Donemus.

BALLOU, Esther W. Suite. ACA.

BERNARD, Emile (1843-1902). Divertissement, Op. 36. Durand, c. 1890.

BLATTNER, O. Two American Sketches. Witmark, 1942.

BYRD, William. Pavane. Andraud.

_____. Suite in D. Ms., Lib. Cong.

CAPLET, Andre (1879-1925). Suite Persane, 1900. Ms., Curtis Inst.

165

CASADESUS, Francis (1870-1954). London Sketches.
Deiss, 1916; Salabert, 1924.

ENESCO, Georges (1881-1955). Dixtet, Op. 14 (D). Enoch.

GIPPS, Ruth. Seascape. Fox, 1961.

JADASSOHN, Salomon (1831-1902). Serenade, Op. 104.
Andraud.

KOZELUCH, Leopold Anton (1747-1818). Harmonie. Simrock.

LILIEN, Ignace (1897-1964). Sonatine Apollonique, 1939.
Donemus.

MELIN. Menuet Badin. Evette; Andraud.

MENGELBERG, Misja. Hello, Windy Boys. Donemus

MOREAU, Lèon (1946-   ). Nocturne. Ms., (V).

MOUQUET, Jules (1867-1946). Symphonietta, Op. 12 (C).
Lemoine.

RAFF, Joachim. Sinfonietta, Op. 188 (F). Kistner, 1876.

SCHMITT, Florent (1870-1958). Lied et Scherzo, Op. 54,
1910. Durand.

SCHRECK, Gustav (1849-1918). Divertimento, Op. 40.
Br. & H, 1905; AMP.

SPORCK, Georges (1870-   ). Paysages Normandes.
Pfister, 1907; Andraud.

STAMITZ, K. Divertimento I (B^b). Mann. Musik.

_____. Divertimento II (B^b). Mann. Musik.

_____. Divertimento III (B^b). Mann. Musik.

TANEIEV, Alexander Sergeievitch (1850-1918). Andante.
Mc & M; Leeds.

TANSMAN, Alexandre (1900-   ). Four Impressions.
Leeds.

WASHBURN, Robert.   Concertino for Two Wind Quintets.
    PP, Jan. 1970.

WHETTAM, Graham.   Symphonietta.   Wolfe.

FLUTE, OBOE, CLARINET, HORN, CONTRA BASS

ROSETTI, F.   Parthia fur die Jagd.   Offentl. Wis. Bib.

FLUTE, ENGLISH HORN, CLARINET,
BASSOON, HORN

SAINT-SAENS, Charles Camille.   (arr.)   Bacchanale.
    Andraud.

FLUTE, OBOE, ENGLISH HORN,
CLARINET, BASSOON

SCARLOTTI, Domenico.   (arr.)   Pastorale.   Schott; Ricordi.

FLUTE, BASSOON, 2 HORNS, TYMPANI

IPPOLITOV-IVANOV, Mikail M.   Dans la Mosquee.   Ms.,
    (HO).

PICCOLO, ENGLISH HORN, BASS CLARINET,
BASSOON, HORN

MILHAUD, Darius (1892-   ).   Symphonie, No. 5, 1922.
    Un. Ed., 1922.

PICCOLO, ENGLISH HORN, TRUMPET,
2 TROMBONES

MAXFIELD, Richard (1927-   ).   Structures for Ten Wind
    Instruments, Op. 23.   Ms., (V).

CLARINET, BASSOON, CONTRA BASSOON,
HORN, TRUMPET

MASEK, (Maschek), Vincent (1755-1831). Parthia (E^b).
   Ms., (V).

OBOE, CLARINET, BASSOON, HORN, CONTRA BASS

REIZENSTEIN, Franz (1911-). Serenade, Op. 29, 1951.
   B & H.

ENGLISH HORN, 2 VIOLINS, VIOLA, CELLO

POULENC, Francis (1899-1963). Mouvements Perpetuels.
   Chester.

CLARINET, BASSOON, HORN, CELLO, CONTRA BASS.

HARTMANN, Emil (1836-1898). Serenade, Op. 43. Ries
   & Erler.

E^b CLARINET, TRUMPET, TROMBONE, CELLO, CONTRA BASS

HINDEMITH, Paul (1895-1963). Kammermusik, No. 3.
   Schott.

2 TRUMPETS, TROMBONE, HORN, TUBA

HAMILTON, Jain (1922-). Sonatas and Varients. Schott.

NAGEL, Robert (1920-). Divertimento for Ten Winds,
   1951. ACA.

PERSICHETTI, Vincent (1915-). Serenade, No. 1.
   Mc & M.

SEAR, W. E. Antiphony. Ms., (V).

TRUMPET, TAMB., STRINGS

PIERNE, Gabriel. Farandolle. Baron.

TRUMPET, VIOLA, 2 CELLO, CONTRA BASS

MILHAUD, Darius (1892-   ). Concerto d'Ete (Viola solo).
Heugel, 1952.

2 VIOLINS, VIOLA, CELLO, HARP

BIRTWISTLE, Harrison (1934-   ). Tragoedia. Un. Ed.

DESTENAY, E. Op. 12 in E^b. Hamelle, 1906.

KAHN, Erich Itor (1905-1956). Actus Tragicus, Op. 12,
1956. Bomart; ACA.

_____. Petite Suite Bretonne, 1936. ACA.

2 VIOLINS, VIOLA, CELLO, TYMPANI

RIETI, Vittorio. Madrigal in Four Movements. Andraud.

2 VIOLINS, VIOLA, CELLO, CONTRA BASS

ANGERER, Paul. Cogitatio. Doblinger.

BRITTEN, Benjamin (1913-   ). Sinfonietta, Op. 1.
B & H.

DUBOIS, Theodore (1837-1924). Dixtet (Clarinet in E^b).
Heugel, 1909.

FICHER, Jacobo. Dos Poemas, Op. 10. Fleisher.

FLEGIER, Andre (1846-1927). Dixtet. Grus, 1890; Lemoine, 1903; Baron.

GHEDINI, Georgio Federico (1892-1965). Doppio Quintetto,
1921. Ms., (V).

HONEGGER, Arthur. Pastorale d'Ete. Andraud.

JACOB, Gordon (1895-   ). Diversions. Oxford Univ.
Press.

KLINGLER, Karl. Variationen (A). Priv., Berlin, 1938.

LALO, Edward V. A.   Two Aubades.   Andraud; Heugel.

LALO, Edouard (1823-1892).   Aubade, 1871.   Heugel.

MOÓR, Emanuel (1863-1931).   Suite, Op. 103.   Salabert, 1913.

PIERNE, Gabriel.   (arr.).   March of the Little Fauns. Andraud.

RAWSTHORNE, Alan (1905-   ).   Concerto for Ten Instruments, 1961.   Oxford Univ. Press.

REICHA.   Diecetto, 1828.   Baron.

_____ .   Gr. Symphonie de Salon, 1827.   Ms. , Paris Cons.

_____ .   Gr. Symphonie de Salon.   Ms. , Paris Cons.

SEARLE, Humphrey (1915-   ).   Variations and Finale for Ten Instruments, 1958.   Schott

Addenda

Woodwind Quintets

ALARD, Delphin. (arr. Tomas). L'Argonesa, Op. 42. Lib. Cong.

ARENSKIĬ, Antoniĭ S. (1861-1906). (arr. Findlay). Berceuse Op. 30. Cundy-Bettoney, 1959. Lib. Cong.

AVSHALOMOV, David. Two Pieces for Wind Quintet, 1966. Programmed by U. S. Air Force Band.

BACH, J. S. (arr. Orem). Boureé. Presser, 1940. Lib. Cong.

_____. (arr. Gordon). Prelude, Cantata 106. Southern Music. Lib. Cong.

_____. (arr. Gordon). Sarabande and Gavotte. Cundy-Bettoney, 1958. Lib. Cong.

_____. (arr. Hirsch). Fugue in C (or. B^b). Ditson, 1937. Lib. Cong.

_____. (arr. Von Kreisler). Prelude and Fugue, WTC no. 4. Southern Music, 1966. Lib. Cong.

BARNES, Clifford P. Robbins Collection of Classics for Woodwind Quintet. Robbins, 1961. Lib. Cong.

BEETHOVEN, L. Van (arr. Brearly). Bagatelle Op. 119, no. 1. Mills, 1966. Lib. Cong.

_____. (arr. Trinkaus). Divertimento Op. 12, no. 2. Witmark, 1933. Lib. Cong.

_____. (arr. Cheyette-Roberts). Larghetto, Sym. no. 2. C. Fischer, 1935. Lib. Cong.

171

_____. (arr. Stark). Quintet from Sextet, Op. 71. C. Fischer. Lib. Cong.

_____. (arr. Philadelphia WWQ). Quintet from Sextet, Op. 71. Presser, 1964. Lib. Cong.

_____. (arr. Nakagawa). Quintet from Sextet, Op. 71. Ms. Lib. Cong.

_____. (arr. Taylor, L.). Rondo from Op. 10, no. 2. Cundy-Bettoney, 1957. Lib. Cong.

_____. (arr. Scott). Piano Sonata Op. 49, no. 19. Waterloo Music Co., Waterloo, Ont.

BIZET, Georges. (arr. H. Elkan). Quintet from Carmen. Henri Elkan, 1956.

BOYD, Charles. (1875-   ). Suite for Woodwinds. Witmark, 1933.

BRAHMS, Johannes (1833-1897). (arr. Huffnagle). Cradle Song. Gornston, 1947.

GAM, N. Suite of Children's Pictures. NACWPI.

GODARD, Benjamin (1849-1895). (arr. Trinkaus). Gique. Kay & Kay, 1935.

GREFRY, Andre (1741-1813). (arr. Buvinger). Dance Legere. M. S. Lib. Cong., 1936.

GRIEG, Edw. (1843-1907). (arr. Trinkaus). Rigaudon. Kay & Kay, 1933

_____. (arr. Trinkaus). Erotikon, Op. 43, no. 4. Kay & Kay, 1935.

_____. (arr. Fischer). Voglein, Op. 43, no. 4. Ditson (Boston), 1934.

_____. (arr. Cafarella). Norwegian Dance. Volkwein, 1951.

HAMM. Round, 1969. NACWPI.

HAYDN, F. J. (1732-1809). (arr. Perry). Divertimento. B & H, 1942.

_____. (arr. Holmes). <u>Menuetto</u> (Sym. 2). Barnhouse, 1935.

_____. (arr. Holmes). <u>Minuett</u> (Sym. 11)

_____. (arr. Meek). <u>Largo.</u> Ditson, 1938.

_____. (arr. Long). <u>Quintet, No. 1.</u> Southern Music, 1961.

_____. (arr. Kesztler). <u>Fuvú sötôs.</u> Val. Zen., 1965.

HEUSSESTAMM. <u>Instabilities for WW Quintet.</u> Probably Seesaw.

HOFF, Don. <u>Gebrauchs Music.</u> Programmed by Iowa Univ. Quintet.

HOLLIGER, Heinz, "H" for Woodwind Quintet. Mentioned in N. Y. Times.

LEMARC, Edwin H. (1865-1929). (arr. Trinkaus). <u>Andan-tino.</u> Kay & Kay, 1934.

MacDOWELL, Edw. (1861-1908). (arr. Hall). <u>To a Wild Rose.</u> Schmidt, 1948.

MENDELSSOHN, F. (arr. Cafarella). <u>Song without Words, No. 62.</u> Wolkwein, 1957.

_____. (arr. Del Jesu). <u>Song without Words, No. 67, no. 1.</u> White-Smith, N. Y., 1951.

MORAWECK, Lucien. <u>Childrens' Sketches,</u> 1961. Lib. Cong.

MOZART, W. A. (arr. Pillney). <u>Fantasy, K. 594.</u> Br. & H., 1966.

_____. (arr. Campbell-Watson). <u>Allegro Concertante.</u> Witmark, 1932.

_____. (arr. Buvinger). <u>Deutscher Tanz.</u> M. S. Lib. Cong., 1936.

_____. (arr. Bryant). <u>Divertimento, No. 12, K252.</u> Jos. Williams, London, 1956.

_____. (arr. Rottler). Divertimento, No. 12, K 252. Leuckhart, 1968.

_____. (arr. Rottler). Divertimento, No. 16, K 289. Leuckhart, 1968.

_____. (arr. Rottler). Quintet (c) - K. 406. Leuckhart, 1967.

_____. (arr. Klickmann). Minuet (Sym. 40). ABC Standard, 1936.

_____. (arr. R. Taylor). March (from Figaro). Wynn Music, Berkeley, Cal., 1961.

_____. (arr. Hirsh). Rondo (from K 375). Ditson, 1937.

_____. (arr. Snieckowski). Quintet (from K 422). Wydawn, 1961.

MUELLER, Florian (arr.) Three Transcriptions for Woodwind Quintet. Camara, 1960. Lib. Cong.

ROMANCHENKO, K. (arr.) P'esy dlia Kvinteta. Muzyka, 1965. Lib. Cong.

TAYLOR, Ross W. (arr.) The Ross Taylor Woodwind Quintets (18 arrs.) Southern Music, 1967. Lib. Cong.

TSCHAIKOWSKY, P. I. (arr. Nakagawa). Three Dances. A. M. P. 1968.

_____. Sleeping Beauty. Mockba, 1963. Lib. Cong.

_____. (arr. Lychenheim). Melody, Op. 42, no. 3. C. Fischer.

_____. (arr. Trinkaus). April, Op. 37, no. 4. Kay & Kay, 1935.

_____. (arr. Trinkaus). June, Op. 37, no. 6. Kay & Kay, 1935.

VOXMAN, Himie, ed. Ensemble Repertoire for Woodwind Quintet. Rubank, 1960. Lib. Cong.